DYNAMIC EDUCATIONAL LEADERSHIP TEAMS

From Mine to Ours

Matthew Jennings

Rowman & Littlefield Education
Lanham • New York • Toronto • Plymouth, UK

Published in the United States of America
by Rowman & Littlefield Education
A Division of Rowman & Littlefield Publishers, Inc.
A wholly owned subsidary of The Rowman & Littlefield Publishing Group, Inc.
4501 Forbes Boulevard, Suite 200, Lanham, Maryland 20706
www.rowmaneducation.com

Estover Road
Plymouth PL6 7PY
United Kingdom

British Library Cataloguing in Publication Information Available

Library of Congress Cataloging-in-Publication Data

Jennings, Matthew
  Dynamic educational leadership teams : from mine to ours / Matthew Jennings.
    p. cm.
  Includes bibliographical references.
  ISBN-13: 978-1-57886-847-6 (cloth : alk. paper)
  ISBN-10: 1-57886-847-5 (cloth : alk. paper)
  ISBN-13: 978-1-57886-848-3 (pbk. : alk. paper)
  ISBN-10: 1-57886-848-3 (pbk. : alk. paper)
  ISBN-13: 978-1-57886-901-5 (electronic)
  ISBN-10: 1-57886-901-3 (electronic)
 1. Educational leadership—United States. 2. School management and
organization—United States. 3. Group work in education—United States. 4.
Meetings—United States—Planning. 5. Teachers—Professional relationships—
United States. I. Title.
  LB2805.J424 2008
  371.2—dc22   2008013412

∞™ The paper used in this publication meets the minimum requirements
of American National Standard for Information Sciences—Permanence of
Paper for Printed Library Materials, ANSI/NISO Z39.48-1992.
Manufactured in the United States of America.

TABLE OF CONTENTS

FIGURES AND TABLES

FIGURES

TABLES

PREFACE

You can learn a lot about an organization by listening carefully to the words that are used. The way people in a school or district speak to others inside and outside of the system says a lot about their beliefs. There are two particular words that may seem innocent, but in reality represent beliefs limiting the progress of schools and districts. Those words are "my" and "your."

"*My* teachers could never do that." "*Your* students did very well on the test." "The teachers in *my* department are very good at using technology." "The students in *your* school have very supportive parents." These statements imply ownership at the wrong level.

All of "our" teachers and all of "our" students perform their work in all of "our" schools. Until we adopt this belief, educators will continue to do what is best for the part of the system they represent. Decisions will continue to be made and actions will continue to be taken that may not promote the success of the organization as a whole.

At best, in a culture of "my" or "your" an individualistic structure will exist. Educators will work in isolation to accomplish goals unrelated to the goals of other educators. At worst, relations among

educators will turn competitive. Believing there are limited rewards or resources, educators will strive to reach their goals at the
expense of other educators. Neither competition nor individualism
will lead to schools capable of meeting modern-day challenges.

To meet the challenges presented by the development of the
world economy and the changing nature of students and society requires a collaborative approach. If we are to provide our students
with the best possible education, then we must choose to interact
in a way that makes the best use of the organization's resources.
This choice begins at the top of the hierarchy in schools and districts.

Leaders with positional power play a powerful role in influencing and shaping the actions of the personnel throughout the system. How the official leaders of the organization interact influences the nature of interactions among the employees in the
system. If they want employees to collaboratively strive for what is
the best for the school or district, then they must be the first to
shift from the focus on "mine" to the focus on "ours."

When followed in a disciplined manner for an extended period
of time, the strategies described in this book will lead to this
change. Traditional leadership teams will become dynamic ones,
capable of achieving continuous improvements in the quality of
learning and teaching. The future of our students and schools depends upon it.

1

INTRODUCTION TO LEADERSHIP TEAMS

A house divided against itself cannot stand.

—Abraham Lincoln

It is a Thursday afternoon on a typical school day in October. Two high schools, each with similar characteristics, begin leadership team meetings at the same time. Yet the members of these meetings have vastly different experiences. First, let us consider Mike's experience.

Mike is the department chair of Smithtown High School's social studies program. As he enters the principal's conference room he takes a seat at one of the chairs surrounding a small circular table. Seated around the table are the other high school subject-area department chairs and the principal of the school.

After some brief social exchanges, the weekly meeting begins on time. The agenda item up for discussion is the district's disappointing performance on a recently administered state-mandated assessment. The district had not performed as well as expected on the writing section of the assessment. The language arts department chair brought this issue to the school leadership team, hoping they could correctly diagnose the problem, generate alternatives, select one, and develop a plan of action. Everyone had thoroughly reviewed the data prior to this meeting.

For approximately the next hour, the group engages in a passionate dialogue that to an outsider might appear similar to a debate. No one at the table looks to blame anyone else. Instead, the group openly engages in dialogue and debate about the nature of the problem as well as potential solutions. During the dialogue there is criticism of ideas, but this criticism is neither intended to be nor is taken personally by the team members. Everyone speaks; no one holds back.

An outsider observing this group would be hard pressed to differentiate who is the department chair for each of the subject areas. The members of this group function as equals. They do not defer to the authority of the principal. His suggestions and ideas are as thoroughly and thoughtfully scrutinized as those of the other group members.

Near the end of this meeting, the group agrees to the implementation of a concrete plan. This plan represents a synthesis of some of the ideas presented during the discussion. The group agrees to place on hold specific departmental staff-development experiences so that professional development can focus on incorporating effective writing-across-the-curriculum activities.

Before leaving the meeting, going clockwise, each person states his or her responsibilities as they relate to the formulated plan. In addition, they identify those individuals not present at this meeting who must receive information regarding the decisions made. They all agree on what and how they will communicate the information to the rest of the staff.

Completing the meeting in a little over an hour, the team members leave feeling energized by the new direction they have established. Mike and his fellow team members are optimistic about the potential success of their plan of action. This is a typical leadership team meeting at Smithtown High School. Contrast this with Jason's experience in the following example.

As the department chair for English at Jonesville High School, Jason has been required to attend school leadership cabinet meetings once a month since he joined the district two years ago. Before leaving his office Jason takes a few minutes to joke with one of the secretaries. His jokes focus on an exchange of creative ideas he could use to avoid attending today's meeting. In reality the laughter, resulting from the creativity of excuses, only helps Jason temporarily deal with his true feelings of despair and dread about having to attend this meeting.

It isn't that Jason doesn't have respect or appreciation for his colleagues. One on one he values the interactions he has with the principal, assistant principal, and his fellow department chairs. In fact, he feels fortunate to be surrounded by such talented and knowledgeable individuals. In their respective roles, each of these colleagues demonstrates the ability to competently perform his or her responsibilities. However, when they assemble into a group for a leadership team meeting the experience is both depressing and demoralizing.

Few people come to the meetings on time. Often the reason for this is that they wait outside the conference room for their "allies" before entering. Having worked with their allies to create a strategy for the items on the meeting agenda, these coalitions are certain to find a place at the table in which they can sit next to one another. As the principal leads the group through the items on this agenda, most of the group members do their best to avoid speaking. When pressed to share their opinions, they often tell the principal what they think he wants to hear.

The exception is the department chair with the most seniority in the district. She frequently offers her opinion on any topic. When she begins to speak, everyone, including the principal, becomes visibly frustrated. To cope with her long and often loosely related rants, some of the group members engage in side conversations or do work they brought with them in anticipation of her long-winded sermons. Occasionally one or two of the group members engage in veiled personal attacks of her knowledge and skill.

When these meetings end, Jason is exhausted from exerting the effort required to maintain appearances. He learned quickly that the real discussions occur in subgroups after the team meeting. It is then that the back-channel politics and personal attacks thrive. He does not want to become the subject of these postmeeting critiques, so he does his best to avoid taking any risks during the meetings. If he does have a potential solution to a problem raised at the meeting, he will bounce it off his wife when he gets home at the end of the day. This is how he reassures himself that he would have meaningful contributions to make if the circumstances were different.

Having survived this day's meeting, Jason returns to his office resentful of the time wasted. Immediately upon entering his office he is confronted with a significant number of issues that require his immediate attention. He knows that if he had not been in the leadership team meeting he could have already dealt with these issues. However, having been at the meeting for the past two hours, he would now need to stay late into the evening if he were to get things in order for the next day. As he washes down two aspirin with a glass of water, he finds himself wondering why the principal even has these meetings.

One meeting results in productive outcomes and energized leaders. The other meeting results in no identifiable outcomes and staff members that feel discouraged. Why might these experiences be so vastly different?

FROM TRADITIONAL TO DYNAMIC

Teams operate along a continuum of effectiveness (Katzenbach & Smith, 2003). Traditional leadership teams operate at a lower level of effectiveness on this continuum. Members of traditional leadership teams work together even though they realize minimal benefit from doing so. Tasks completed by the members of this type of team require little if any joint efforts. As a result, members do not take responsibility for anyone's achievements but their own. Individual efforts remain the focus of reward and recognition.

A traditional leadership team has a single leader that is in charge of directing members' participation. The membership of a traditional leadership team is fixed and exclusive. To be a member of the leadership team, a person must hold a specific position within the organization. Leadership team meetings may or may not occur on a regular basis, but typically are as infrequent as possible.

There are no structured opportunities for processing the quality of a traditional team's efforts. Furthermore, there is no group attention focused on improving interpersonal and communication skills so that the team may become more effective. Jason is a member of a traditional leadership team.

At the higher end of the effectiveness continuum are dynamic leadership teams. *A dynamic leadership team is a group of three or more educational leaders that share responsibility and accountability for the achievement of common organizational goals.* Importantly, members of dynamic leadership teams willingly set aside individual, departmental, or building needs for the greater good of the school or district. Dynamic leadership team members share compelling goals that serve to motivate them to work toward something beyond their individual achievements.

Coupled with this common, compelling purpose is the belief that individuals are accountable for their actions as well as the actions of the others on their team. Rewards and recognition are contingent on group performance. Members of dynamic leadership teams share leadership responsibilities based on the nature of the task. Also, while there is a core group of leadership team members, others will be added to the team on a temporary basis if their expertise is necessary for task completion.

Dynamic leadership teams realize the importance of regular face-to-face interactions. Their meetings are regularly scheduled, focused, and purposeful. During these meetings, team members exhibit agreed-upon behaviors. Improvement on these communication and interpersonal skills is part of a continuous improvement process that is a top priority for dynamic leadership teams. Lastly, dynamic leadership teams reflect on both their task work and their teamwork. These teams celebrate the group's achievements and make improvements in their processes in order to be more successful in future endeavors. Mike is a member of a dynamic leadership team. Table 1.1 provides a comparison between traditional and dynamic leadership teams.

Table 1.1.   Comparing Traditional and Dynamic Leadership Teams

	Traditional Teams	*Dynamic Teams*
Interdependence	Goal achievement and rewards/recognition are based solely on individual effort.	Goal achievement is based on the collective, coordinated efforts of team members. Rewards and recognition are contingent on individual and group performance.
Accountability	Accountable for the results attained as part of their individual responsibilities.	Accountable for both the results attained in their individual areas of responsibilities and the results attained by the team.
Group Membership	Fixed and exclusive.	Core group with members added based on the task to be achieved.
Group Behaviors	Ignored unless they become problematic. Focus on problems associated with individual personalities.	Explicitly focused on and developed. Focus on group dynamics and interactions.
Frequency of Interactions	Infrequent and/or irregular.	Frequent and regularly scheduled.
Group Processing	No structured opportunities for structured reflection.	Regularly scheduled structured-reflection activities.

Like the members of Mike's group in the opening example, members of dynamic leadership teams achieve well beyond what could be achieved by individuals working alone. While it is hard work, members of dynamic leadership teams frequently enjoy the process of completing their tasks. Unfortunately, dynamic leadership teams are rare in education (Johnson & Johnson, 1994). Based on observations, research, discussion with colleagues, and personal experience, it is far more common to serve on a traditional leadership team like Jason's.

THE IMPORTANCE OF DYNAMIC LEADERSHIP TEAMS

Creating dynamic leadership teams is a process that requires significant amounts of both time and effort. Group members need time and experience working together if they are going to develop into an effective team (Johnson & Johnson, 1994). Furthermore, there is a set of principles that must be planned for and followed in a disciplined way in order to create the conditions for effective cooperation (Katzenbach & Smith, 2003). With the demands and pressures placed on leaders at every level of schools, why should the investment of time and effort in this area be a priority?

To answer this question it is helpful to revisit the teams introduced at the beginning of this chapter. The principal of each of these schools was the individual primarily responsible for initiating and structuring these leadership teams. Reginald, the principal of Mike's school, and Alan, the principal of Jason's school, share many demographic and professional similarities. However, one of the major differences between them is their underlying beliefs about the purpose of leadership teams.

Decision Making

In his previous role as a high school department chair, Reginald had seen many decisions made by the high school principal and members of the central office staff that did not make sense when implemented at the classroom level. Frequently the decisions required actions that did not take into account the unique nature of each subject area or classroom. Thus initiatives failed, resulting in an ever-increasing divide between upper-level leadership and the staff members in the district. Reginald believed that having a team consisting of departmental-level leaders would make it possible to reach decisions representative of the wide range of interests and viewpoints present in the school. Ultimately decisions would be better because they would be based upon the diverse perspectives of the stakeholders affected by them.

As a leader, Alan believed the important decisions should be made by the principal of the school. He believed leaders choosing to delegate decision-making authority lacked decisiveness as well as the strength required to be in charge. Furthermore, unless he took responsibility for making the important decisions, Alan did not believe he could develop a high-quality school. He was the individual that would be held accountable for the results of the decisions, so he was going to exercise the authority to make them. The main role of the members of his leadership team was to understand what he wanted done and then make sure it happened.

Reginald had always been frustrated by the tendency of upper-level leaders to develop and implement mandates he and his colleagues were simply expected to follow. Frequently he was bewildered by the reason or need for these decisions. Of course he would comply with these mandates, but rarely did he do it with a high degree of commitment. Reginald's experience had led him to believe that when school- and district-level leaders collectively play a role in shaping decisions, both groups better understand and are more apt to support the decisions made.

Alan believed that decisions should be followed because they were issued by those with the authority to make them. He expected unquestioned compliance with his decisions. According to Alan, anyone that did not listen to the orders resulting from his decisions was not a team player and did not belong as a staff member in his school. A primary reason for selecting the members to serve in positions as departmental chairs was his perception that because of their loyalty to him, they could be counted on to follow through.

Problem Solving and Task Completion

Both Reginald and Alan realized that the combination of decreased funding and the increased expectations resulting from federal and state mandates meant their schools were entering an era of unprecedented challenges. Reginald knew that meeting these challenges would require creative solutions to new and more difficult problems. Reginald believed that composing a leadership team with district- and school-level leaders, each of whom possesses different skills, knowledge, and perspectives, could result in the type of creative organizational solutions the district would require in order to thrive in this new era.

Alan believed that competition among the various department chairpersons would result in the greatest chance of meeting the new challenges. To get the best out of his leadership team members, Alan focused on publicly recognizing and rewarding them for the improvements they initiated in their departments. He consistently pointed out the successes achieved by individual leadership team members at their regularly scheduled meetings.

Developing creative solutions to difficult challenges is a positive beginning. However, as Reginald had learned, the real challenge often comes with the implementation of those ideas. Initiating and sustaining change efforts in education is frequently an emotionally challenging task for school leaders. Reginald believed that if his leadership group was going to take on and then persist in the difficult tasks associated with improving their school, they would require positive social support. In addition, Reginald had always found the pressure of letting down respected colleagues much more difficult than feelings of personal disappointment.

Alan believed that persistence and initiative were qualities individuals either did or did not possess. Using a team approach to encourage work toward task completion was something he had never considered. Leadership team members did their tasks because they were directed to complete them. If they did not complete them successfully, that fact should and would be reflected in their annual performance evaluations.

Coordination and Consistency of Programs and Services

Reginald believed that ultimately it is staff members and students that pay the price when their leaders cannot or will not work effectively with leaders in other areas of the school or district. Reginald could vividly remember a situation in which the director of special education had difficulty working effectively with the principal of an elementary school. Due to the fact that these two individuals communicated poorly and infrequently, the special and general education teachers in that building received different messages. As a result these teachers were unsure of their performance expectations and the eventual goals they were expected to achieve. Going in different directions with different expectations for their performance, teachers provided students with vastly different experiences. Reginald's viewpoint was that through frequent, accurate communication the school's programs and services would become and remain more cohesive and consistent.

Alan also believed that communication was important for the achievement of cohesion and consistency of programs and services. In order to achieve this communication and coordination, Alan told his leadership team members what was expected and how it was to be achieved. If there were interpersonal difficulties among team members, it was their responsibility to work them out. Team members were expected to work together as professionals and while it would be nice, it was not necessary for them to like one another.

Morale and Productivity

Reginald was very concerned about maintaining stability among leadership team members in the high school. Through his career Reginald has seen the profession of school leadership grow increasingly stressful. He did not want to lose any of his leadership team members due to feelings of frustration or isolation. Reginald reasoned that people want to be part of something positive and effective. If they are part of a leadership team that produces meaningful results and promotes feelings of being both valued and appreciated, they will stay in that setting. It is difficult to leave a situation in which you are known and cared about.

Alan's opinion was that his school district paid very well. Those in leadership positions receive generous compensation and are fortunate to hold their positions. If anyone on his leadership team is foolish enough to want to leave for a position elsewhere, Alan is certain he could easily replace them with someone else. After all, according to Alan, if you are paid well then accountability and expectations should both be high. If a person could not accept that fact, or could not handle the stress, then being a leadership team member in his school was not the right fit for that person.

Attitudes toward Collaboration

Lastly, Reginald was concerned with his leadership team's success because experience had taught him that when leadership teams are ineffective, group members develop skeptical attitudes about the use of teams in general. Dysfunctional leadership teams breed negative attitudes about the use of teams in other parts of the organization. At a time when collaboration for the development of professional communities is considered essential for the continuous improvement of schools, Reginald knew he could not afford to allow this attitude to permeate the beliefs of his leadership team members.

Alan did not make any connection between the leadership dynamics among his team members and their attitudes toward teamwork in other parts of the organization. In fact, he considered the
whole emphasis on professional learning communities to be just
another educational fad. Alan believed that what really mattered
was what teachers did with their students in their classrooms.

A summary of the Importance of Dynamic Leadership Teams

- Decisions represent the interests and viewpoints present
  within the school system.
- Participation in decision making leads to increased support
  for, and better understanding of, the decisions made.
- The varied skills, knowledge, and perspectives of team members result in creative organizational solutions.
- Willingness to persist on difficult tasks increases.
- District and school programs and services become more cohesive and consistent.
- Leadership team members feel a sense of belonging and support from colleagues.
- Leadership team members improve their attitudes toward
  collaboration in other areas of the organization.

Barriers to Creating Dynamic Leadership Teams

Reginald's leadership team is dynamic. However, this was not always the case. In fact, despite his strong beliefs, early in his tenure
as the principal, Reginald almost abandoned the leadership team
concept. He had led many teams before, so he could not understand the resistance he was receiving from the members of this
group. Reginald was especially frustrated with this situation because this leadership group was composed of seasoned leaders, all

of whom had extensive experience designing and leading collaborative groups in their respective classrooms and departments. What Reginald had not considered was the unique aspects of leadership teams in schools and districts. His frustration would have been far less if he had been aware of the five distinct reasons school and district leadership teams have difficulty attaining high levels of performance.

Membership in the leadership team does not constitute a major activity for group members. The principals, directors, and other leaders composing these teams spend most of their time and focus most of their attention in their schools or with their departments. The time they do spend with the leadership team is typically limited to regularly scheduled meetings and occasional retreats.

During meetings of traditional leadership teams the individual responsibilities and goals of group members are frequently a higher priority to the individuals than the group's goals (Katzenbach, 1998). As a result, issues that offer the opportunity for a genuine team effort are frequently addressed from a departmental or school perspective without consideration for the larger organizational system.

Time is a scarce commodity for school leaders. When leadership groups gather, their members often strive to minimize the amount of time spent together without sacrificing the effectiveness of the discussions and decisions made. However, time is one of the elements required for groups to become dynamic teams. Teams inevitably go through a period of adjustment during which group members learn to work together effectively. During this adjustment period, the effort required of team members will be high and the process will be less efficient than traditional leadership teams.

A leadership team that applies a basic set of principles, in a disciplined manner, over a period of time will outperform a collection of individuals (Katzenbach & Smith, 2003). However, it is difficult to convince school and district leaders that the long-term benefits of becoming an effective leadership team are worth the initial investment of time required.

Dynamic leadership teams have established mutual accountability among their members. However, in traditional leadership teams the performance contract that exists is usually between each group member and the team leader. For example, each of the department chairs is accountable to the principal and not to the other members of the leadership team.

As a result, leadership teams have difficulty attaining high levels of performance because individual roles and responsibilities serve as the primary focal points for evaluating performance results. Without a sense of mutual accountability leadership team members are likely to have a low degree of commitment toward achieving the team's desired collective performance outcomes.

The preponderance of experience most school leaders have had is in hierarchically organized, single leader–led environments. This model has worked successfully enough for them to reach the leadership level in a school or district. As a result, school and district leaders are both familiar with and have learned to trust this model. School and district leaders are less skilled and frequently far less comfortable working within team-based approaches to leadership.

Lastly, the extra performance potential leadership teams provide comes in part from the skill mix of the group's members. In traditional school or district leadership teams it is the position of the individual and not his or her knowledge or skill that determines their role in the group. All of the individuals in certain job categories are on the team regardless of what they can or cannot contribute to the team's performance.

Ego, visibility, and even personal commitments and compassion can make it difficult to exclude or include certain staff members from a leadership team. This aspect of leadership teams frequently deprives them of the group composition necessary for effective performance.

Barriers to Effective School and District Leadership Teams

- Membership in leadership teams is not a major responsibility for team members.
- Time is a precious but limited commodity for school administrators.
- School administrators are only accountable to the leader of the district.
- School administrators are comfortable working in hierarchical, single leader–led environments.
- Group composition and roles are determined based on position, not skills or knowledge.

SOLUTION

In an environment characterized by complex challenges and constant change, effective teamwork at the top of the hierarchy in any school or district is crucial. Unfortunately, where dynamic teams are needed the most is the same place where it is often the most difficult to attain them.

How do leadership teams get there? The good news is that the solution is neither expensive nor overly complicated. What is challenging about this solution is that it requires adherence to a set of principles and strategies in a disciplined way over an extended period of time.

This is bad news, because in an era of public ranking of schools and high-stakes testing it is difficult for leaders to focus on solutions that do not produce immediate results. Additionally, it is difficult for leaders to "give up" power and trust the capacity of others with the current pressure resulting from state and district accountability measures.

A leadership team will not succeed unless it is composed of members with the expertise and skills required for meeting the team's performance goals. Furthermore, the size of the team must be small enough for members to interact constructively. Task requirements and size limitations frequently require making difficult decisions. However, if a team is ever to become dynamic, the official team leader must begin the process by making sure the right people are on (or off) the team. As obvious as this may sound, it is a common failing among school and district leadership teams. Composing leadership teams is the subject of the next chapter.

Early in its existence, a dynamic leadership team must establish a common and compelling purpose for working together. This common and compelling purpose will serve as fuel to sustain the investment of time and emotional energy required to develop and maintain behavioral cohesiveness. It will also serve as the glue that will keep team members from moving in different directions at cross-purposes. Developing a common and compelling purpose is the subject of chapter 3.

Dynamic leadership teams do not emerge until group members become behaviorally cohesive. In order to reach this goal, leadership team members must establish minimum levels of interpersonal trust, engage in productive conflict, commit to decisions and plans of action, hold one another as well as themselves accountable for their actions related to achieving those plans, and maintain a focus on collective results.

These synergistic behaviors are interrelated, with one serving to reinforce the others. In other words, if one of these behaviors is lacking in the group, it will become very difficult to focus on achieving collective results. For example, a team that does not engage in productive conflict will be characterized by members that lack commitment to the decisions made.

The achievement of these synergistic behaviors is a process that is never ending. Instead, the team must regularly and systematically reflect on their collective and individual strengths and weaknesses. Chapters 4 through 8 address each of five synergistic team behaviors.

Reflection, goal setting, problem solving, and decision making are activities that frequently occur in meetings. For good reasons, many school leaders do not like meetings. Overly ambitious agendas, no agendas, out-of-control discussions, or no clear direction can make even the most dedicated employees want to call in sick on the day of a meeting. Meetings can be improved through more effective planning and facilitation. This will be the subject of chapter 9.

2

COMPOSING A LEADERSHIP TEAM

> In a good to great transformation, people are not your most important asset. The right people are.
>
> —Jim Collins

As the assistant superintendent of schools, Mrs. Dennis knew that completing a three-year technology plan for the school district would require skills and knowledge the members of the leadership team did not possess. After sharing this belief with the leadership team members, she proposed inviting several technicians and two technology-savvy teachers to the next leadership team meeting. She explained the rationale for her suggestion by stating that these teachers and technicians would work with the rest of the leadership team to develop the required technology plan. What she assumed was an obvious suggestion ended up being met with fierce resistance by several of the school principals.

While these principals could not clearly articulate their rationale for why this was a bad idea, it was obvious from their emotional reaction that they adamantly opposed inviting these staff members.

Caught by surprise, Mrs. Dennis decided to postpone further discussion of this idea for a future meeting.

Compare Mrs. Dennis's experience to that of the assistant superintendent of a neighboring school district. Because he was in a school district governed by the same state mandate, Dr. Davis and his district's leadership team also had to develop a three-year technology plan.

At the next meeting, Dr. Davis brought the issue of completing the technology plan to the members of his leadership team. After a careful review of the tasks required for completing this plan, group members identified the aspects of this task for which they were confident the team already possessed sufficient skills and knowledge. They also identified those aspects of the task for which the team members lacked the necessary knowledge and skills.

After identifying the aspects for which the team lacked skills and knowledge, they discussed who, both inside and outside of the organization, could join the leadership team as a temporary member. A technology teacher, a computer technician, and a parent employed as an information systems manager for a major company were targeted. The group concluded this part of the meeting by deciding who would reach out to those individuals and by when that would be completed.

LEADERSHIP TEAM COMPOSITION
IN PUBLIC SCHOOLS

In his book *Good to Great*, Jim Collins states, "The transformation from good to great begins with getting the right people on the bus (and the wrong people off the bus) and then figuring out where to drive it (2001). The key point being asserted is that decisions about who will be on a team must precede questions about what the team will accomplish. This concept is important, yet it presents some unique challenges in public schools.

The composition of leadership teams in public schools is not as easily changed as it can be in industry. In many cases, the school leader enters the position with many of his or her subordinate leaders already holding tenure in their position. In some cases, policy mandates require leaders to compose teams with elected members or volunteers. In public schools, the official team leader is often very limited in his or her ability to select individuals for leadership positions.

Compounding this problem is the common expectation held by educational leaders that all of the individuals holding a certain job title should be a member of the leadership team. For example, all of the principals expect to be members of the leadership team because of their official position, not because of their potential contribution to the team's efforts. Even though they may have little knowledge and skills to contribute to an issue, these leaders are involved simply because they are members of the group.

Membership on a leadership team simply because of position within an organization creates two problems. First, team membership based solely on job title may not provide teams with the complementary skills required to complete a task. In the example at the beginning of this chapter, even though the team was composed of all of the official school district leaders, they did not possess the necessary level of knowledge or skills related to technology. Without this knowledge, the team would have difficulty effectively completing their task.

Second, membership on a leadership team based solely on position may result in teams that are too large to be effective. Including all of the positional leaders may lead to teams that are so vast that communication and coordination become very difficult.

Despite these constraints, the team leader must do everything possible to create a team composed of the right number of the right people. The first reason this is so important is because smaller teams are more likely to develop the common purpose, goals, approach, and mutual accountability characteristic of real teams (Katzenbach & Smith, 2003).

Second, teams consisting of members with the appropriate expertise and skills are more likely to meet their purpose and performance goals (Johnson & Johnson, 2006). Thus, if we want to create leadership teams that achieve the desired results, team leaders may need to make informed yet difficult choices.

Team Size

The official leader of a school or district team usually has some discretion in determining the size of his or her leadership team. If this is the case, what is the optimal number of people composing a leadership team?

In his analysis of the effect of group size on group productivity, psychologist Ivan Steiner determined that the potential productivity of a group (what a group can theoretically produce if member resources were used optimally) increases as size increases (Steiner, 1972).

However, this productivity increase occurs at a decreasing rate. In other words, each new group member contributes something to group productivity, but not as much as the previous group member contributed. Increasing a group from three to four has a far greater impact on group productivity than adding a twelfth person to an eleven-member group.

Steiner also found that groups never perform at their potential level of productivity because of what he referred to as "process losses." Process losses include coordination and communication challenges, motivational issues, and other inefficiencies that occur when people work together in groups. Process losses also increase with size, but they do so at a much faster rate (Hackman, 2002). Thus, the actual productivity of a leadership team is defined as its potential productivity minus the process losses.

According to Hackman (2002), the actual productivity of a team increases as group size increases to up to five members. Actual group productivity then decreases for every member added after five. Thus, all things being equal, when making decisions about the size of a leadership team, smaller teams are potentially more effective than larger teams.

However, there is a problem associated with small leadership teams. While they are potentially more productive, they may not include all of the relevant stakeholders. Without both clear understanding and buy-in from building and department leaders, complex decisions requiring a high level of coordination will not be adequately implemented. Yet ensuring all of the relevant stakeholders are represented on the team is likely to result in a large, politically correct group that is incapable of generating a productive outcome. So what is the solution?

The solution to this problem is the identification and selection of a core group of team members representative of the various stakeholders within the school or district. This core group of four to six members remains in place as the leadership team for all meetings and activities.

These core group leadership team members must stay in close communication with those they represent on the team. They are charged with representing their viewpoints at leadership team meetings, as well as communicating the outcomes from those meetings.

Core group team members must understand that the potential mix of members will expand when necessary in order to provide all of the essential task-related skills. For example, suppose the school leadership team was discussing a plan for integrating technology into the curriculum. After some discussion, the core members of the school leadership team determine that they do not possess the necessary understanding of computer networking or hardware issues for developing this plan. However, the district's technology coordinator is an expert in this area. Even though he is not a standing member of the district's leadership team, because of his technical skills, he is asked to serve as an adjunct team member while the focus is on this topic.

Those who perceive membership on the team as a source of status, like the principals in the example at the beginning of this chapter, may be resistant to these additions. However, these team members must be made to understand that membership on the leadership team is not about hierarchical standing in the organization; rather it is about achieving organizational results.

Key Points Related to Team Size

- All else being equal, smaller teams are more effective than larger teams.
- Four to six representative core members should be permanent members of the team.
- Team membership must expand to include others when task-related skills or knowledge are missing.
- Those viewing team membership as a status symbol may resist adding other members.

IDENTIFYING CORE LEADERSHIP TEAM MEMBERS

Selecting the core group members for a leadership team is a critical yet difficult balancing act. Not only must these individuals represent a larger constituency within the school or district, they must also be well respected for their abilities and character. In addition, they must possess the necessary communication and collaboration skills required to work effectively with other members of the team. These attributes make up the minimum requirements for members of the core group of a leadership team.

A dynamic leadership team goes beyond these minimum requirements to purposefully strike a balance between members that are either too similar or too different from one another. Research evidence indicates that when working on complex problems that require some degree of creativity, groups are more effective when they are composed of individuals with diverse types of skills, knowledge, abilities, and perspectives (Johnson & Johnson, 2006). Complex problems requiring creative solutions are the types of tasks most school and district leadership teams confront on a regular basis.

On the other hand, if the core group of a leadership team is excessively heterogeneous it may have a rich diversity of talents and perspectives, but may be unable to capitalize on using them. Team members may be so different in how they think and act that they are unable to communicate and coordinate with one another competently.

Furthermore, when the diversity of team membership is too extreme, the group may have difficulty achieving the level of group cohesion required for effective team performance. Low levels of group cohesion have been linked to increased levels of member absenteeism and turnover as well as lower levels of satisfaction among group members (Johnson & Johnson, 2006).

The challenge for the individual responsible for selecting the core group members of a leadership team is to balance carefully between too much similarity and too many differences. One possible source of diversity is demographic characteristics. More specifically, the team may benefit from being composed of individuals from both genders, a range of age groups, and/or different ethnic backgrounds (Johnson & Johnson, 2006).

A second source of diversity is an individuals' skills and abilities. Individuals with expertise in different content areas may approach problem solving differently. For example, an individual with a science background may approach a problem in a methodical manner. An individual with a background in the performing arts may approach solving that same problem through an intuitive approach.

Likewise, the team benefits from being composed of individuals experienced in serving students of different demographic characteristics. For example, when school-related issues are discussed, individuals experienced working with students that have disabilities or limited English proficiency may raise concerns that otherwise may not have been considered. At a district level, an individual with a background in elementary education will likely see issues differently than an individual with a secondary school background.

A final source of diversity is individual personality characteristics. While there are many dimensions that can be used to divide people into distinct personality types, two are particularly relevant to the success of leadership teams. These two dimensions are risk taking and people orientation.

Risk taking can be viewed along a continuum from high-risk-taking behavior to low-risk-taking behavior. People closer to the high-risk-taking end of the continuum can be characterized by a number of behavior patterns. Typically, they are perceived to be assertive and directive. High-risk takers exhibit a take-charge attitude and hold strong opinions. Individuals that are high-risk takers display the behavior of being impulsive in their decision making. Lastly, these individuals enjoy taking the lead and seek to control the direction of a group.

Individuals that display low-risk-taking behavior exhibit the opposite behavior patterns. Typically, they act in a manner that is reserved and calculated. Their actions are characterized as consistent and predictable. These are the individuals that can be counted on to complete their responsibilities. Instead of making statements about issues and people, low-risk-taking individuals tend to ask questions. Unlike high-risk takers, these individuals have no interest in influencing the thoughts and behaviors of the members of the group.

A group composed entirely of high-risk takers would run the risk of making decisions and taking actions without adequate analysis of the situation. A group composed entirely of low-risk takers might plan and analyze for so long they miss critical opportunities. Additionally, if the group contained individuals near the extremes of each continuum, their vastly different approaches would likely lead to interpersonal tension. If possible, the core group of the leadership team should contain a balance of people with moderate-risk-taking tendencies toward both ends of the continuum.

Much the same as risk taking, the dimension of people orientation can also be described along a continuum. More specifically, individuals range from high to low people orientation. Those with a low people orientation prefer to work alone. Typically these individuals are task focused. When dealing with people, those with low people orientation are formal and reserved. They do not display emotions and prefer that colleagues do the same when interacting with them.

Those with a high people orientation thrive on working in groups. They love to collaborate with colleagues on projects and ideas. In fact, the task is frequently less important to them than the interpersonal relationships among the group members. Typically these individuals are enthusiastic and entertaining. Lastly, those with a high people orientation display strong communication skills.

If a group consisted solely of individuals with high people orientation, they would likely have a good time, but not get much done. On the other hand, a group entirely composed of those with low people orientation would probably not function as a group for long. Additionally, those at the extreme ends of the continuum on people orientation would at a minimum annoy one another and would likely be unable to communicate with each other effectively. Therefore, the ideal core group membership of a leadership team will be composed of individuals with a moderate degree of people orientation toward both ends of the continuum.

In the early stages, a heterogeneous team will often experience more difficulties than a homogeneous team. Members of a heterogeneous team will struggle to determine the most effective ways to work together. However, if members make it through these early difficulties they are likely to produce outcomes that are significantly better than those generated by more homogeneous teams (Hackman, 2002). Thus, the team leader must carefully avoid falling into the trap of creating a team that will work smoothly and harmoniously at the expense of producing valuable outcomes for the organization.

Key Points Related to Diversity among Core Team Members

- At a minimum core leadership team members must represent a larger group, be well respected for their abilities and character, and have effective communication and collaboration skills.
- Dynamic leadership teams go beyond these minimum requirements to ensure the core group members are moderately diverse.
- Potential sources of diversity include demographic attributes, skills and abilities, and personality characteristics.

STABILITY OVER TIME

Should the core group of a leadership team remain the same for an extended period of time? The answer to this question is a clear and resounding yes. Teams with stable membership outperform teams that constantly need to deal with the arrival of new members and the departure of old ones (Hackman, 2002). This is the case even if all of the group members possess group skills and have previously participated in effective groups (Johnson & Johnson, 2006).

There are at least four reasons why this is true. The first reason is that over time team members develop familiarity with one another. Thus, they are able to shift their attention and energy from getting acquainted to working on the task.

Second, over time team members learn each other's strengths and weaknesses. With this knowledge the team has an increased capability to capitalize on members' knowledge and skills.

Third, team members learn how to effectively deal with those members lacking teamwork and/or task-related skills. They become able to do this without excessively disrupting the team's progress toward achieving desired objectives.

Finally, over a period of time group members typically build a shared commitment to the team and a high degree of caring about one another's success. In other words, the level of commitment goes beyond civility and teamwork to a genuine desire to help the other team members achieve both their personal and professional goals.

Put simply, group members need time and experience working together in order to develop into an effective team. Yet for a variety of reasons current leadership team members may leave the organization. When this happens new members will be added to the leadership team.

The advantage of these additions is the new skills, knowledge, and perspectives these team members bring with them. Furthermore, to the extent that the newcomer stimulates discussion about how the team operates, their introduction may lead to improvements in the team process. The disadvantage of adding new team members is that time and energy must be spent orienting new team members and learning to work effectively with them. Usually this must be done without sacrificing the pace and focus of the team's task work.

At the beginning, newcomers often will be anxious about their role in the group. Thus, they tend to act passively and demonstrate high levels of dependency and conformity. According to Moreland

and Levine (1989), these behaviors actually increase the new-comer's acceptance by established group members. A newcomer may be perceived as a threat to the team because he or she brings a new, objective perspective. The passive approach adopted by most newcomers reduces the potential threat of criticism of the team and thereby encourages acceptance of the new member (Levi, 2007).

After the initial socialization phase has been completed, the individual will enter the maintenance stage. At this point, the individual is fully committed to the group and the group has accepted the individual as a full team member. However, even though the individual is a full member of the team, there continues to be an ongoing process of negotiating his or her role and position in the group.

In sum, turnover of team members can have positive and negative effects on a team (Levine & Choi, 2004). Yet because of the amount of time required to achieve this goal as well as the temporary loss of team cohesion, it is important to limit the number of people entering or exiting the leadership team.

Key Points Related to the Stability of Team Membership

- Teams composed of membership that is stable over time will outperform teams in which membership changes frequently.
- Effectively adding new team members requires the time and energy of current team members. For this reason, changes in team composition should be limited.

DISRUPTIVE TEAM MEMBERS

To this point, the assumption has been that the official team leader will have discretion in deciding who will serve on the leadership team. When team members are elected or appointed this is not the case. Thus, there is an increased possibility that a team member will not have the skills required for competent teamwork. He or she may be unwilling or unable to learn effective interpersonal skills. What should be done in these situations?

First, it is necessary to make sure this attribution is correct. People tend to view behaviors that are disruptive as reflecting some problem with the person who exhibits them (Hackman, 2002). However, sometimes those behaviors reflect the perspective of another group not represented on the team.

For example, suppose a team consists of five teachers and one parent. Consistently that parent is acting in a way that appears disruptive to the other members of the team. It is possible that this person is in fact difficult.

Yet it is also possible that the person is operating from an alternate perspective that characterizes most parents. If this possibility is not explored, the team runs the risk of ostracizing the parent. As a result, the team avoids dealing with intergroup issues that should be addressed, not suppressed.

Another potentially destructive misattribution derives from the psychological phenomenon known as splitting (Smith & Berg, 1987). In emotionally charged settings, people may deal with their uncertainties and ambivalences by splitting the positive and negative affect they are experiencing into separate parts. All of the positive affect is attributed to one person (the hero) and all the negative affect is assigned to another (the bum).

This phenomenon is especially destructive in teams composed of a few members with distinctive demographic characteristics. Those with distinctive demographic characteristics are the most likely to be viewed as being unable to work in groups. As a result, they are assigned most or all of the blame for collective failures. This impulse to scapegoat an individual when the team encounters difficulties can be quite strong.

Compounding this problem is the fact that the scapegoated team member often starts to behave in accord with his or her teammates' expectations (Hackman, 2002). A self-fueling spiral whose outcomes do no good for either the person or the team has been set in motion.

Assuming the attribution is correct and the person truly does have poor interpersonal skills, the team must find a way to reap the individual's potential contributions while at the same time minimizing the risk to the team and its work. Teammates working collaboratively with this person can frequently make significant progress in helping the individual learn basic teamwork skills.

If this peer coaching does not have the desired impact, then the team should pursue the option of isolating or working around the individual. This way the team can complete their tasks without being impeded by the actions of the disruptive team member. This is especially difficult to do when the individual has extraordinary task-related skills.

By working around or isolating the individual, the team is in effect dismissing that person from the team. That is a drastic action, only to be taken after everything else team members can think of has been attempted.

Key Points Related to Difficult Team Members

- Before labeling a team member as being difficult, it is important to make sure that attribution is correct.
- Team members should attempt to coach the individual in the necessary teamwork skills. If this fails and there are no other alternatives, the team may need to isolate or work around the difficult individual.

As stated throughout this chapter, the value of the team approach to leading schools or districts depends heavily upon the composition of the team. The individual responsible for determining team membership must make several critical decisions regarding team composition.

All of these decisions must be made with a keen awareness of the political ramifications for each choice. Importantly, political pressure cannot replace skills and knowledge if the goal is to create a team that will achieve the desired organizational results.

Making sure the right people are on the team is a critical first step. Developing a shared, meaningful purpose for working together is the next step. Developing this common and compelling purpose is the subject of the next chapter.

3

CREATING A COMMON AND COMPELLING PURPOSE

No wind favors him who has no destined port.

—Montaigne

Driving to work, Samantha began to reflect on the day ahead. Most of the day would be spent in a leadership team meeting with all of the district's administrators. As a brand new middle school principal, she found these meetings frustrating. As a teacher, her middle school teaching team meetings usually had a clear sense of purpose. When they met, their goals were to coordinate curriculum and instruction, parent communication, and behavior management strategies. These goals shifted depending upon the circumstances, but accomplishing one of them was always the reason they met. Furthermore, these activities had a direct and usually significant impact on the education of the students on their team.

Samantha even thought about the committees she had served on. These groups had a different focus than her middle school teaching team. Yet they always had something important to accomplish. At times it was a decision which would impact upon the school or district. Other times it was a recommendation for the principal to consider. Either way, there was a meaningful task the group needed to accomplish.

It was this sense of a shared purpose that Samantha found missing from the activities of the leadership team. When they gathered together, the team occasionally had interesting discussions. In the more interesting meetings, the discussions would take on the characteristics of a debate among the team members. Usually, the primary task accomplished was the superintendent sharing information and delegating tasks for team members to accomplish.

She quickly learned that the outcome of most of these meetings was more work for her and her administrative colleagues. Maybe that was why she had come to resent these meetings. Samantha didn't mind hard work. She just did not see the connection between the assigned tasks and the purpose for the leadership team.

When tasks required the coordination among members of the leadership group, those involved were told to work together to complete them. The directive to work together usually did not lead to truly cooperative efforts among team members.

DEFINING A COMMON, COMPELLING PURPOSE

The leadership team described in the previous example did not share a common and compelling purpose. The members of this group could easily complete their assigned tasks without the assistance of most of the members of the team. Success or failure at the completion of individual tasks served as the basis for rewards and recognition. Furthermore, the superintendent retained the sole responsibility for assigning and then evaluating the quality of task completion.

With no need to work together and existing structures focused on individual task completion, it should come as no surprise that Samantha did not see the shared purpose for this leadership team. Yet this team did serve a purpose.

Like most traditional leadership teams in schools and districts, this team served as the mechanism through which the team leader delegated responsibilities, ensured the sharing of information, and coordinated various activities. Additionally, on occasion the superintendent put a topic on the agenda for discussion. However, after listening to the input of team members he always made the final decision.

Almost everything that occurs during this type of meeting could be done one on one in a meeting between the team leader and the individual team members. It is simply more efficient to gather everyone as a group.

Meetings for this type of team do enable the leader to be certain the same message is communicated to all of the team members. In a time-urgent situation such as a crisis or when the leader really is the most knowledgeable on the issue, this pattern of interaction may be appropriate. Yet by itself, acting in this way will not lead to a dynamic team.

Members of a dynamic leadership team share a common and compelling purpose. This common and compelling purpose is a future state of affairs desired enough by all of the team members to motivate them to collectively apply their various skills and knowledge in order to work toward its achievement. This purpose is important and cannot be achieved by any one member acting on his or her own.

"POWERFUL" GOALS

For a leadership team a common and compelling purpose is translated into action through team goals. In order for these goals to be effective, they must be "POWERful."

> ➤ P—Positively Interdependent
> ➤ O—Operational

➤ W—Worthwhile
➤ E—Explicit
➤ R—Rational

A positively interdependent goal requires group members to believe they are connected with other team members in such a way that they cannot succeed unless the rest of the group succeeds. When a goal is positively interdependent, team members must maximize their own productivity as well as the productivity of all of the other members of the leadership team. Without positive interdependence there is little extrinsic reason for leaders to collaboratively strive for goal achievement.

An operational goal is one for which the results can be both observed and counted. The operational aspect of the goal provides the feedback necessary for the team to formatively and summatively assess their progress as it relates to successful goal completion. Able to assess their own progress, the leadership team can adjust their current and future group processes and task completion strategies to improve team performance.

A worthwhile goal is one that the members of the team perceive to be both challenging and consequential. It is neither too easy to complete nor is it well beyond the current capabilities of the team. In addition, team members see completion of the goal as being relevant to both their individual needs and the needs of the larger organization. When team members perceive attainment of the goal as worthwhile, it energizes and engages them to use higher levels of effort toward goal completion.

Explicit goals are clear and specific. Goals that are considered explicit provide team members with detailed images of the desired outcomes. Every member of the team knows what the goal has been formulated to accomplish as well as how they will know it has been achieved. Knowing the desired outcomes, team members can then select among a range of alternatives for achieving that goal. With appropriate, goal-focused task-completion strategies selected, team members can coordinate and synchronize their actions.

A second characteristic of an explicit goal is that it has a clear deadline for completion that is understood by all of the leadership team members. Establishing a realistic time frame by which the goal is to be completed keeps achievement of that goal a high priority for the group. A deadline that is impossible to meet or excessive will not establish the desired sense of urgency among team members. It is this sense of urgency that enhances the compelling nature of the goal.

The last element of a "POWERful" leadership team goal is that the goal must be rational. A goal is rational when it is based on solid evidence. More specifically, this evidence consists of two parts. First, the reason for selecting the goal must be based on research. What qualitative and/or quantitative data exists to justify the team's efforts toward achieving this goal? If there is no data to support the selection of the goal, then there is an increased probability that the goal will not achieve significant results.

Second, the strategies selected and sequenced for achieving the goal should be research based. Unless there already exists an abundant amount of legitimate expertise within the team members, a careful, comprehensive review of scientifically accepted literature in areas related to the subject of the goal should precede the development of task-completion strategies. Choosing research-based task-completion strategies will also improve the probability of successful task completion.

THE NEED FOR A COMMON AND COMPELLING PURPOSE

Leadership teams frequently do not have a common compelling purpose for working together (Katzenbach & Smith, 2003). This is especially problematic when you consider one unique but frequent challenge faced by this type of team. Most of the team members of a school or district leadership team place a higher priority on the team they represent than on their membership on the leadership team (Lencioni, 2002).

Precedence for the team they represent over the leadership team occurs due to four reasons. First, leadership team members often spend more time with those on their departmental or school-based teams. This time spent together allows interpersonal relationships to mature and develop.

Second, the frequency of communication between colleagues decreases dramatically as the physical distance between them increases (Luecke, 2004). Educational leaders are more likely to communicate regularly with members of their school or department team because they are in close physical proximity to them. Regular communication is another aspect of developing positive interpersonal relationships.

A school or departmental leader with an established tenure serving in a district will likely have interviewed and recommended for hiring many of the staff members he or she leads. This being the case, the third reason leaders hold the interests of a team they represent higher is that they have an increased sense of ownership and investment for that team. Put simply, it is their team.

Lastly, many school administrators simply enjoy being leaders more than they enjoy being followers (Katzenbach & Smith, 2003). Typically, they have risen to a position of influence in the school or district because they excel in settings focused on achieving their individual best results, as well as holding others similarly accountable. These individuals are more comfortable being in charge than they are following or collaborating with others.

Placing a higher priority on the team being led than on the leadership team has predictable but ruinous consequences for the larger organization. Rather than coming together to make the best possible decisions for the entire organization, team members lobby for their own schools or departments. When push comes to shove, leadership team members compete with their teammates rather than collaborate with them.

The foundation of an effective leadership group is the group members' ability to go beyond barter and compromise to embracing the collective pursuit of the best interests of the organization as a whole. A common, compelling purpose built on "POWERful" goals helps lay this foundation.

A second reason for developing a common and compelling purpose is that it encourages leadership teams to remain focused on priorities. Schools as public institutions are subject to the influence of multiple interest groups, each of which frequently has competing priorities.

If schools are going to be successful focusing their efforts on those issues with the greatest possibility for increased student achievement, they must say no to those things that distract from this goal. Having a common and compelling purpose makes it possible to say no to those things that are not supportive of the team's priorities.

Developing a Common and Compelling Purpose

A common misconception is that the school or district's mission statement is the purpose for the leadership team. In reality, most mission statements are too broad and abstract to provide adequate focus for the collective actions of a leadership team. For example, consider the district mission statement of "providing excellence and equity for all students." This is a noble aspiration, but it is difficult to translate into concrete, actionable steps that will guide a leadership team's efforts.

Yet within the mission of "providing excellence and equity for all students" many possibilities exist. The key is to narrow and sharpen the focus from the overall school or district mission to "POWERful" goals. In the example that follows, the process for accomplishing this task is described.

Dana is the recently appointed superintendent of schools for a midsize school district. Approximately a month into her tenure she scheduled a two-day off-site retreat for her leadership team. A week prior to this retreat, she provided her team with a synthesis of achievement data for all of the students in the school district. This synthesis included her disaggregated analysis of standardized test scores, report card grades, attendance rates for teachers and students, disciplinary actions, and drop-out rates. The team was instructed to review this data prior to the date of the retreat.

This district leadership team consisted of four elementary principals, a middle school principal and vice principal, a high school principal and vice principal, four K–12 subject area supervisors, the school business administrator, the director of student services, and the assistant superintendent.

A distinguishing characteristic of this district was its long-held tradition of school-based decision making. This tradition of school-based decision making had led to a lack of consistency and fidelity within school programs. Of particular concern was the problem of each school applying district policies and initiatives in very different ways.

The district was fragmented, and tensions caused by competition among the schools were high. Through this retreat, Dana intended to engage the team in a series of activities she hoped would result in a common and compelling purpose. More specifically, the desired outcome was the development of action plans leading to the achievement of two "POWERful" goals.

She decided that one goal would focus on instruction, and the other would focus on student achievement. While instruction and achievement are clearly related, Dana decided she needed to maintain a focus on both process and results. Dana was convinced this outcome would begin the process of moving from a focus on individual schools toward a focus on the schools as a system.

After conducting a series of nonthreatening, fun getting-acquainted activities, Dana began her introduction to the process of developing a common, compelling purpose. She shared her reasons for why the leadership team needed to have a common and compelling purpose. She followed this with a description of the five elements of "POWERful" goals. Lastly, she described for the group the desired outcomes for this part of the retreat.

After answering questions, Dana proceeded to conduct the first activity. On a whiteboard in the front of the room Dana listed the question *what is the single most important action we can take to improve academic achievement in our school district?*

Next, Dana explained to the team that their task for the next fifteen minutes was to generate as many answers to this question as possible. Prior to telling them to start she reviewed the following guidelines for brainstorming in a group setting:

- Aim for lots of ideas—the more the better.
- Avoid evaluating ideas at this point.
- Build on and add to others' ideas.
- Avoid repeating or trying to sell an idea.
- Welcome and record all ideas.

At this point, Dana used a random method for assigning team members to small groups. Each group was directed to select a recorder who would list the ideas on a piece of chart paper. The chart paper and marker were to rotate to the next team member clockwise after four ideas had been shared. This way the recorder would be able to participate equally in the generation of ideas.

Once fifteen minutes had passed, Dana stopped the group. The pieces of chart paper were taped onto the wall in places where all of the team members could view them. The group was given a short break so Dana could eliminate duplicates as well as combine like answers.

Before introducing the next part of the activity, Dana provided the team with an opportunity to get clarification on any of the items listed that they did not understand. She also checked with them to make sure her combinations for like ideas were accurate and acceptable.

Next Dana posted a piece of chart paper containing a set of guiding questions designed to narrow the number of options. These questions, related to the "POWERful" goals, were:

- Does successful completion of this option require the efforts of all of the leadership team members?
- Is it possible to observe and count the result of this option?
- Is it possible for us to implement this option?
- Does the option draw your energy and attention?
- Do we have evidence that implementation of this option is necessary in our district?
- Do we have evidence that implementation of this option has the potential to make a significant difference in the quality of education for our students?

After reviewing these questions, Dana facilitated a discussion in which group members eliminated options. Beginning with the first question, options were eliminated if the answer to the question was no. Those options remaining at the end of this discussion were those receiving a yes answer to all of the guiding questions.

Next, Dana divided the number of different remaining options (eleven) by three. Rounding up to the nearest whole number, Dana came to the answer of four. Thus, she gave each team member four colored sticky dots. She explained to the group that each of these dots represented one vote that they could place next to the options they favored most.

For the next ten minutes the group silently milled around the room distributing their dots. It turned out that two of the items received no votes. These were immediately crossed off.

Three of the options received less than 25 percent of the possible votes. These items were discussed by the group. Everyone agreed to eliminate two of these three options. However, two of the group members believed the third option from this group was critical. Thus, this option was left on the list for the next vote.

The process was repeated with different colored dots. After this second round, four of the ideas clearly received an overwhelming majority of the votes. Dana listed these four ideas vertically in a column on a new piece of chart paper.

At this point, she initiated a discussion with the group about the criteria to be used for determining which of these options would be selected for implementation. The group decided on the following criteria: amount of professional development required, potential long-term impact, cost, and the amount of instructional time required.

Through questions and discussion, Dana made sure everyone understood what was meant by each of these criteria. In addition, the group discussed and then determined that each of the criteria was of equal value. Therefore none of the criteria were weighted for scoring purposes. Vertical columns were created for each criterion.

Going across the chart and using a scale of zero (not met at all) to five (fully met), each team member privately scored each option against the criteria. Upon completing their scoring, individual team members tabulated their total score for each option. Dana computed an average of the individual scores in order to obtain a team score. One option emerged as the strongest match to the criteria.

As a final step toward selecting an option for the team to implement, Dana used a method called fist-to-five. She began this activity by explaining that there would be three levels for team members to select from in order to express their individual opinions. On her signal, they would show three, five, or no fingers to display their level of agreement and support for this option.

The display of five fingers indicated total agreement and support for the option. The display of three fingers indicated willingness to support the option even though they still held some concerns. A fist indicated the individual would not support the implementation of this option because of serious concerns.

After confirming everyone's understanding of the levels, Dana asked team members to display the appropriate number of fingers. The majority of the team members displayed five fingers. Two of the team members held up three fingers and no one held up a fist.

Those displaying three fingers were given an opportunity to express their concerns. One of the concerns was relieved by the group agreeing to make one minor change. Despite the remaining minor concerns, all of the team members agreed that they had been listened to and understood and that they understood the nature of the option selected. Thus, everyone stated support for the selected option as focus for the development of a team academic achievement goal.

After a short break, Dana refocused the group so they could develop an action plan leading to completion of the goal. During the break, Dana wrote the following goal on the top of a piece of chart paper: By June of 2009, 85 percent of the district's students will write a five-paragraph essay that earns at least a proficient score as measured by the district's writing rubric.

After the break, she reviewed the goal statement with the team to make sure it accurately stated their desired outcome. The team agreed the goal statement was accurate, so Dana drew and then labeled columns titled Action Steps, Responsibilities, Timelines, and Evaluations.

The process for completing the action plan started with the group listing all of the steps necessary for achieving the goal. As group members called out steps, Dana recorded them on self-stick notes. She did this so the steps could be sequenced appropriately.

After making sure the steps were correctly sequenced, the group proceeded to identify and list the leadership team members responsible for completing each step. The group discussed and then decided upon when each of the steps would be started and completed. Lastly, after recording these deadlines the group determined and listed the methods they would use to ensure each action step was successfully completed.

On the second day of the retreat, the group completed the same process. This time the initial question for brainstorming was *what is the single most important action we can take to improve the quality of instruction in our school district?* Having thoughtfully and systematically engaged in the described processes to answer both questions, the leadership team emerged from this retreat having established a common and compelling purpose.

To develop their common and compelling purpose, this leadership team progressed through a series of structured activities. These activities, which are described in detail in the appendix, are:

1. Brainstorming
2. Guiding Questions
3. Dot Voting
4. Decision Matrix
5. Fist-to-Five
6. Action Planning

The power of the team's purpose depends in part on the team's ability to embrace their current reality. If the team either does not know or denies the truth surrounding their circumstances, the goal they select will likely be focused on the wrong targets.

Embracing reality begins with team members having the courage to acknowledge the facts regarding their current situation, no matter how unpleasant those facts may seem. To acknowledge the facts regarding a team's current situation requires systematically gathering and analyzing data.

This data may come from tools designed to understand perceptions and opinions. For example, in-depth interviews, focus groups, and surveys can be used to identify areas of satisfaction as well as opportunities for improvement. Data can also come from tools designed to measure student performance. Standardized, criterion-referenced, and curriculum-based assessments can be employed to determine the strengths and weaknesses of the instructional program. All of this data can be disaggregated by subgroups in order to get an even clearer picture of the team's situation.

It has been my experience that most schools have a tremendous amount of data at their disposal. The problem is not the lack of data. Instead, the problem is the act of rationalizing or avoiding data that team members find unpleasant.

Instead of ignoring or explaining away this data, dynamic leadership teams confront, organize, and analyze it to better understand the reality of their current situation. They do this before starting the goal-setting process so that the team can make thoughtful decisions.

Implementing the action plans developed through the activities described in this chapter requires both individual and mutual accountability as well as the maintenance of a focus on collective results. These behaviors and interpersonal trust, productive conflict, and collective commitment are "synergistic team behaviors." Interpersonal trust, the first of these behaviors, is the subject of the next chapter.

4

BUILDING TRUST

The moment there is suspicion about a person's motives, everything he does becomes tainted.

—Mahatma Gandhi

The superintendent has asked the members of the district leadership team to his office for a meeting. Several days ago the district received a court order requiring the placement of two students classified for special education services in costly out-of-district programs. These unanticipated expenditures along with several other unexpected costs have plunged the district into a difficult financial situation. To deal with this situation, the business administrator and superintendent engage the other members of the leadership team in a discussion focused on the actions that can be taken to reduce current and future costs enough to make it through the remainder of this school year. Donna, an elementary school principal, is part of this meeting. As Donna is sitting in this meeting, her attention begins to wander and she has the following thoughts:

I think we could share the costs of our graduation expenses by rescheduling the dates. If we move our elementary promotion ceremonies one day apart then we could share some of the items we each would need to purchase otherwise. I think we could also look at our schedules and find a way to share current teacher assistants. We probably don't really need to hire another new aide. Do the superintendent and business administrator really think I would bring up these ideas in front of my colleagues? They must not get it. If I bring these ideas up not only will the other principals find all kinds of ways to shoot down my ideas, they will be angry at me for even suggesting them. They still hold a grudge over the last time I spoke during one of our budget meetings about sharing an assistant principal. Maybe if the superintendent and business administrator didn't make us fight so hard for everything during the budget development process we wouldn't be in this position.

Abruptly her focus is drawn back to the meeting when she hears the superintendent say, "Donna, can you think of any additional ideas for helping us get through this situation?" Donna politely replies, "I can't think of any new ideas. I think all of the ideas already mentioned cover just about everything we can do."

DEFINING TRUST

Trust in a dynamic leadership team is defined as *a high level of confidence among the members of the team that their colleagues have positive and honorable intentions*. Realizing that group members have a genuine desire to do what is best for one another and the school district, group members do not feel they need to be overly protective or careful when they are with this team.

As a result, team members demonstrate a willingness to make themselves vulnerable to one another. In addition, they have confidence that their respective vulnerabilities, including weaknesses, skill deficiencies, interpersonal shortcomings, mistakes, and requests for help, will not be used against them in the future.

In groups that have high levels of trust, interactions among members are characterized by the following behaviors:

- Group members freely admit mistakes and weaknesses.
- Group members are honest and straightforward in their communications.
- Group members freely share information and data.
- Group members are loyal to those that are not present.

THE IMPORTANCE OF TRUST
TO LEADERSHIP TEAMS

When the level of trust is low, concern for self-preservation is high. Group members focus their attention and effort on strategy and politics, not the task at hand. The vast majority of time and energy is spent on managing one's own behavior and members' interactions within the group. The tactics and strategies employed when trust levels are low among leadership team members frequently result in wasted time, talent, and energy.

Because team members are reluctant to take risks or offer assistance, meetings of teams with low trust levels are frequently dreadful events that group members simply wish to emerge from unscathed. A frequent response to the demand for attending a meeting of a group characterized by low trust levels is that group members' bodies are physically present, but not their hearts and minds. Team members attend these meetings out of compliance, but they are not committed to giving their talent, creativity, energy, or passion to the team.

Ironically, a common response of many school leaders to low trust levels is the creation of additional systems and structures designed to ensure control. Rather than focusing on improving the organization, team members are forced to focus on multiple layers of approval, excessive paperwork, and regulations.

In turn, these systems and structures prompt behaviors from team members that appear to be untrustworthy. In response to their feelings about the increased demands, they do not complete the necessary paperwork or follow the articulated regulations.

As a result, the leader perceives these behaviors as validation of their initial perception of the need for more bureaucracy. It becomes a vicious downward cycle leading to low levels of morale among team members. The ultimate cost of low trust levels among leadership team members is a high turnover rate among group members.

Lastly, trust is a prerequisite for productive conflict to occur. Without sufficient trust, team members will engage in filtered discussions. Team members will not engage in passionate, unfiltered debate focused on important ideas because they will fear retribution if they say something that is interpreted as being destructive or critical. Without trust, team members will be evasive and possibly even dishonest with one another in their communications.

Trust is the foundation of an effective team. Without a basic level of trust, teams will never achieve high levels of performance. Trust will not necessarily rescue a poor strategic plan, but low trust will almost always derail a good one (Covey, 2007).

A Summary of the Importance of Trust to Leadership Teams

- Team members focus their energy on the task to be achieved and not on the management of appearances.
- Team members commit to giving their talent, creativity, energy, and passion to the team.
- Less bureaucracy is required so more time can be devoted to completing important tasks.
- Team members are honest when they communicate with one another.

BUILDING AND MAINTAINING TRUST

Trust is not a stable personality trait residing within individuals. Rather, trust is a dynamic aspect of the relationships among team members. Trust levels increase or decrease based upon the actions taken by the members of the team. Repeated actions that are considered trusting and trustworthy will lead to the establishment of high trust levels among team members.

Without interpersonal risk, trust will not develop among the members of the team. More specifically, for trust to develop someone has to risk being vulnerable and then see whether others will abuse that vulnerability. Vulnerability in a team setting is exhibited when group members demonstrate openness. *Openness is the sharing of information, ideas, thoughts, feelings, and reactions to the issue the group is pursuing*. In our example, Donna was not open because she did not take the risk of sharing her ideas or feelings.

This openness can be met by either confirmation or rejection. Confirmation is displayed through acceptance. *Acceptance is the communication of high regard for another group member as well as his or her contributions to the group's work*. If Donna had expressed her idea and it had been met with sincere interest and thoughtful consideration she would likely have felt a sense of acceptance. This would in turn reduce her anxiety and fears about demonstrating vulnerability in the future.

Acceptance does not equate to agreement. Through their language and actions team members can disagree with the content of another team member's idea and still demonstrate respect for that individual and his or her contributions. For example, imagine if Donna had shared her idea for combining graduation expenses. In turn team members thoughtfully examined the positive and negative aspects of the proposal. Eventually the team rejects the idea for valid reasons that Donna had not considered. The careful and genuine consideration of her ideas would likely be enough for Donna to continue feeling accepted by the members of the group.

Rejection is demonstrated when team members use ridicule or disrespect in response to another's openness. Making a joke at the expense of a group member, laughing at personal disclosures that are serious, moralizing about behavior, and remaining silent when a response would be appropriate are all behaviors that can be perceived as demonstrating rejection. Once perceived, rejection will silence that group member and erode the trust within the relationships.

Distrust is also created when a group member refuses to share his or her thoughts, information, conclusions, feelings, and reactions. In the example, Donna may not have shared her thoughts because none of the other principals shared their ideas. If she had shared her ideas at this point, she might have felt overexposed and vulnerable.

Even though it takes time to build trust, it is a relationship quality that can be destroyed quickly and easily. For example, imagine the situation in which the principal of one school tells a few of her school's staff members about personal information shared by another principal in a leadership team meeting. Both the nature and the source of the information get back to the principal who had originally shared that information. This betrayal of confidence is probably enough to establish distrust among these individuals regardless of how many trusting interactions they had previously.

Broken trust creates disappointment and pain. There are situations like the one above in which trust may not be able to be restored. The betrayal may be so severe that trust is shattered, and there is no way to restore it. By far the best approach is to never violate trust in the first place. Instead of taking it for granted, leadership team members must build, value, cherish, protect, and preserve trust.

When a violation of trust does occur, the person responsible must quickly and genuinely acknowledge the mistake. They must apologize for their behavior and make an attempt to fix any of the damage they have caused.

Restoring trust may be difficult and painful and may take a long time. However, making it happen must become a top priority for any team member that has broken the trust of another member of the leadership team.

Important Points about Building Trust

- Trust does not reside within people; rather it is a dynamic aspect of relationships.
- Interpersonal risk is required for building trust.
- Acceptance of team members' openness leads to increased trust.
- Rejection of team members' openness leads to decreased trust.
- Trust takes a long time to develop, but can be destroyed quickly.

THE OFFICIAL TEAM LEADER'S ROLE

Through language, attitude, and actions, the official team leader plays a critical role in developing a high trust level within a leadership team. One way he or she does this is by being the first to take the risk of being open with the other members of the group.

The team leader must have the courage to risk being open with the other members of the team without having any guarantee of success. The leader must be the first to take this leap of faith and demonstrate vulnerability without knowing whether that behavior will be respected and reciprocated.

Admitting a mistake, requesting assistance, or indicating a lack of certainty to the members of a leadership team will likely begin the process of getting team members to do the same.

When spoken honestly, the words, "I made a mistake," "I need your help," and "I'm not sure what we should do" are crucial if team members are to get to the point where they stop wasting their time and energy thinking about what they should say or what their colleagues' intentions are.

However, this display of vulnerability must be genuine or it will risk being perceived as an attempt to manipulate the feelings and emotions of others. The perception of acting in a manipulative manner will result in a decrease in trust levels.

Group leaders should not expect people to open up within the team environment quickly. Respect the fact that team members will proceed at different paces and will likely move gradually.

The idea of putting oneself at risk for the good of the team does not come naturally and goes against what members have learned about what it takes to achieve personal success. Simple icebreaker activities like sharing about hobbies, outside interests, and favorite movies or music are nonthreatening starting points.

The treatment of those that are not present in a meeting is a telling indication of the way we would be treated if we were not present. When a team talks about someone behind their back, it causes those who are present to think the same will be done to them when they are not there. This certainly does not build trust!

The team leader must not engage in or allow others to engage in negative talk about someone that is not present. A good general rule to guide behavior in group settings is to only speak about the person as if they were present.

Once people do begin to open up, the team leader must create an environment that does not punish the display of vulnerability. The leader can accomplish this by modeling supportive, coaching-oriented responses to team members' admissions of weakness or failures. Additionally, the team leader must intervene when any member of the group displays behaviors that ridicule or reject the open behaviors of others.

When questioned or challenged, the leader must respond in ways that are not defensive. Instead of becoming angry or defensive, a team leader can listen thoughtfully and acknowledge any valid points made. This models the ability to admit mistakes and comfort without demonstrating uncertainty or needing help.

Everyone makes mistakes. It is not whether or not you make a mistake, it is what you do once one has been made that is important. Being humble is the path that will inspire trust among leadership team members.

Leaders that inspire trust among team members demonstrate a willingness to extend trust to others. Neither does this mean extending trust indiscriminately or unwisely, nor does it mean acting like you trust someone when you don't. Appropriately extending trust requires analysis of the situation, risk, and character and competence of the individuals involved.

However, when team members have earned trust, the leader should extend it to them abundantly. This means not only giving the individuals the responsibility, but also the authority to get a task done. While involving some risk, this action is one of the fastest ways a leader can create a high-trust culture among the members of a leadership team.

Lastly, the leader must avoid consulting with some team members and not with others before reaching a decision. This action has a tendency to intensify competition among team members for the leader's attention. As a result, dissension occurs among team members and fragmentation within the team increases. When the team leader conducts group-related business with certain members outside of the leadership team setting, trust within the team inevitably deteriorates. Team issues must be addressed with the whole team.

Official Team Leader's Role in Building Trust

- The leader must be the first group member to demonstrate vulnerability-based trust.

- Be patient and realistic with expectations for team members' demonstration of openness.
- Speak about individuals only as if they were present.
- Model supportive responses to admissions of weakness or failure. Intervene if anyone attempts to ridicule or reject the open behavior of others.
- Model willingness to admit mistakes and comfort with uncertainty or needing help.
- Extend appropriate trust to team members.
- Conduct team-related business with the entire team.

Having established a basic level of trust among group members, engaging in productive conflict becomes possible. More specifically, when trust levels between team members are high, task-related conflict is less likely to lead to relationship conflict (Levi, 2007). Productive conflict in leadership teams is the subject of chapter 5.

5

PROMOTING PRODUCTIVE CONFLICT

Difference of opinion leads to inquiry and inquiry to truth.

—Thomas Jefferson

Consider two leadership teams each presented with the task of reviewing the effectiveness of the current district policy on retaining students at a grade level. Team A has a strong desire to preserve harmony among team members. Team B has a strong desire to make the best decision possible.

Team A holds a meeting. As the superintendent listens, each team member presents his or her viewpoint on this issue as well as their supporting rationale. Six of the eight group members express a viewpoint in favor of the current policy. These individuals challenge the viewpoints of the two minority members. Even though these two members expressed doubts about the effectiveness of the current policy, they quickly change their point of view to one that is in agreement with the majority.

Contrast this with Team B's meeting. The members of this team also express their viewpoints and supporting rationale. Even though the majority of the team members are in favor of the current policy, the two group members with concerns advocate for changes. They engage in a process of argument and counterargument that goes back and forth as the individuals attempt to persuade one another. However, they don't argue blindly. Instead, team members also actively seek to understand each other's viewpoints. Eventually the group agrees to synthesize some of the ideas discussed into a new policy statement.

If this is the model of decision making Team A applies to important issues on a regular basis, they will efficiently reach superficial agreements. On the other hand, Team B will struggle with decisions. However, this struggle will likely yield a broader understanding of the issues, the generation of more alternatives, and the selection of a more comprehensive solution with sustainable results. Dynamic leadership teams engage in the type of conflict characterized by the description of Team B.

DEFINING PRODUCTIVE CONFLICT

Productive conflict among leadership team members can be defined as *discussion of the advantages and disadvantages of proposed actions, with the intent to create novel solutions to problems of critical importance to the school or district.* More specifically, the discussion characteristic of productive conflict is not characterized by pride and competition among team members. Team members are neither trying to get their way, nor are they trying to win. Instead, team members engaged in this type of conflict are pursuing the best possible solution to any problem or dilemma.

These discussions are not personality-based attacks designed to be mean-spirited or hurtful. Destructive fighting and interpersonal attacks are never acceptable behaviors on a leadership team. Teams that engage in productive conflict have interactions that are characterized by:

- group members actively seeking out the perspective and opinions of all group members,
- group members stating their opinions on issues without holding back due to fear of retribution or rejection,
- group members freely expressing support for ideas as well as doubt and objections,
- two-way communication occurring between all group members,
- critical issues and topics being placed on the "table" for discussion.

THE IMPORTANCE OF PRODUCTIVE CONFLICT TO LEADERSHIP TEAMS

Productive conflict is essential for any leadership team that hopes to become dynamic. Productive conflict results in issues being discussed thoroughly. Alternatives to a proposal or suggestion are more likely to be carefully considered from a variety of viewpoints. Thus, the quality of the decisions made tends to increase when leadership teams engage in productive conflict.

In addition, productive conflict is efficient. When a conflict is avoided in one setting, it tends to arise again in a future setting. Important conflicts often do not just simply disappear. Teams that avoid conflict waste time because they tend to revisit issues repeatedly without ever coming to resolution. Not only is this inefficient, it is frustrating and tends to lower morale among team members.

Teams that avoid conflict often do so in a misguided attempt to promote harmony. This artificial harmony frequently results in a dangerous tension among team members. When team members do not openly debate and disagree about important ideas, they often resort to private attacks in the staff lounge or hallways.

These back-channel attacks are usually far worse and more harmful than spirited conflict over issues of importance. Teams that embrace the norm of engaging in productive conflict consist of members that force themselves to say everything that needs to be said when the time is appropriate. As a result there is nothing remaining that needs to be said behind closed doors.

Lastly, productive conflict in which group members believe their ideas have been thoughtfully and genuinely considered will result in increased member commitment to the implementation of decisions. Regardless of the outcome reached, most people who believe their opinions and perspectives have been listened to will commit to seeing a group's decision through to completion.

Value of Productive Conflict to a Leadership Team

- The quality of team decisions improves.
- The team becomes more efficient with their meeting time.
- There are fewer "meetings after the meeting," and back-channel attacks are unnecessary.
- Team members have increased commitment to the implementation of decisions.

AVOIDANCE OF CONFLICT

Even though productive conflict is important, it is frequently avoided by leadership teams (Cloke & Goldsmith, 2005). Instead, leadership teams frequently engage in concurrence-seeking behaviors (Johnson & Johnson, 2006).

This concurrence-seeking behavior is characterized by group members acting in ways that inhibit discussion. By inhibiting discussion, the group members can avoid disagreement and arguments. As a result of this desire to emphasize agreement, groups displaying concurrence-seeking behaviors avoid the rational appraisal of alternatives.

Why might this concurrence-seeking behavior be so prevalent? There are at least three reasons why leadership team members avoid engaging in productive conflict. First, any conflict has the inherent potential to result in either constructive or destructive outcomes. Thus, if members fear the conflict may create divisiveness and hostility they are likely to avoid engaging in this type of interaction.

Second, because of cultural norms that are common in our society, conflict is perceived to be harmful and as something that should be avoided (Johnson & Johnson, 2006). The general feeling among most school personnel is that a well-run group is one in which there is minimal conflict among members. Conflict in our culture is not viewed as a powerful force for improving the quality of decision making and problem solving.

Third, most school personnel do not have training in the effective use of the skills required for effectively engaging in productive conflict. For conflict to be managed positively, at a minimum, team members need to learn how to disagree skillfully and engage in rational argumentation. These are not skills included in most pre- or in-service training programs.

Reasons Leadership Teams Avoid Conflict

- Team members' fear of potentially destructive outcomes.
- Cultural views that conflict is negative.
- Team members' lack of skill for engaging in productive conflict.

PROMOTING PRODUCTIVE CONFLICT

Most educational professionals have learned to speak carefully and within accepted boundaries. Yet rarely will a group of individuals with diverse experiences, perspectives, values, and expectations commit to focusing on collective action without encountering significant conflict. Dynamic leadership teams acknowledge and accept this discomfort. Additionally, they push past their discomfort because they know it is necessary for making the best possible decisions for the school or district.

Inherent in any conflict is the potential for positive or negative outcomes. What determines the outcome of most conflicts is the conditions under which they occur and the methods in which they are managed. Teams that engage in productive conflict explicitly establish norms for how conflicts will be viewed and managed.

Early in the life cycle of a school or district leadership team, the group must acknowledge the fact that in order to be effective and efficient, conflict will be necessary. Establishing the belief that conflict focused on ideas is essential for the team's success is the first step a team can take toward encouraging productive conflict. Instead of viewing a conflict as a win-lose situation, the team must reframe conflicts as problem-solving opportunities.

Furthermore, conflict becomes an opportunity for learning and growth when it is viewed by the team as an "it" rather than a "who." These are two example norms a team could adopt in order to become more conflict-positive. However, each team must discuss and decide upon their behavioral expectations for how conflict will be managed within their team. The appendix contains an exercise for leadership teams to use for creating their own positive-conflict norms.

Another important step a school or district leadership team can take toward facilitating productive conflict is the provision of relevant information to meeting participants in advance. Most school personnel feel more confident presenting their opinions if they have had time to review background information. The ability to form opinions and supporting rationale prior to a meeting will typically lead to a higher-quality discussion on any issue.

Frequently one of the most challenging aspects of engaging in productive conflict is establishing clarity among group members on the nature and magnitude of the issue or problem. Being provided with relevant information in advance and having established norms supportive of productive conflict will not lead to a fruitful outcome if team members are discussing separate issues, but believe they are discussing the same thing. Thus, being clear and accurate about the nature and magnitude of the issue will make productive conflict possible.

Consider the following scenario. A district leadership team is wrestling with their professional development plan for the remainder of the current school year. To define the issue, team members make clear and concrete statements describing their concerns regarding the nature of the issue. For example, one of the principals says, "There are six half-day staff-development sessions proposed in our current plan. Attendance at each of these sessions requires teachers to miss class." As additional statements are made, one of the team members charts them on a piece of flip-chart paper. This process continues until the team members run out of statements.

Next, the group removes those items from the list that require resources or authority beyond the group's control. For example, this group takes off their list the concerns related to one of the topics in the professional development plan. State regulations require that every district staff member receive the content of that particular topic during the course of the current school year.

The statements remaining are redefined to include a description of both the desired and the actual state of affairs. For example, the principal's original statement is restated as, "Currently there are six half-day staff development sessions that teachers must miss class time to attend (actual), I would prefer to have three half-day sessions during the school day and three sessions after school (desired)." No one argues or attempts to solve the problem at this point.

Upon completing this process, the team has a discussion in order to decide upon the statement members agree is the most accurate description of the group's concern. After combining aspects of several of the statements, the group reaches a decision. Now they can move forward fairly certain that there is a common understanding of the nature and magnitude of the issue.

It is tempting to quickly progress toward generating solutions. However, a dynamic leadership team will resist this temptation. Instead, they will first generate a clear, agreed-upon definition of the issue or problem. The process used in the scenario, which is described in the appendix, is a structured process to be used for achieving this goal.

A group's ability to engage in productive conflict is related to the level of interpersonal trust among group members. More specifically, teams with high levels of trust among members can tolerate task-related conflict and use the conflict productively (Levi, 2007). While the development of interpersonal trust can be accelerated through the use of the strategies previously described, it will take time.

Thus, having established positive norms for conflict-related behaviors, providing information in advance, and using structured procedures for defining a problem may still not lead to productive conflict within a team.

Until the necessary level of trust has been developed, the team leader may need to structure these discussions. For example, the district school board is presented with the dilemma of overcrowding in the schools. They have taken the time to both review the available demographic information and ensure shared understanding of the nature of the issue. Having reached the point in which two viable alternatives have emerged, the group engages in the following process.

Using a method of random assignment, one half of the board is assigned the alternative of redistricting the schools. The other half of the board is assigned the option of adding on to the existing facilities through school construction. Both subgroups know that they are responsible for advocating in favor of their assigned alternative regardless of their personal beliefs or feelings.

Between meetings, each subgroup researches its position. They prepare a presentation that is designed to convince the other group of the validity of their alternative. At the meeting both subgroups present their case.

At this point, the subgroup members switch roles. More specifically, group members present the best possible case they can for the alternative they were initially assigned to oppose. This is done to ensure group members see both the advantages and disadvantages for each option.

Upon completing these presentations, an open discussion ensues. Team members state their points of view and refute one another's positions. Eventually a solution emerges in which some construction must be done, but the amount is minimized by reconfiguring the grade levels attending the various buildings in the school district. The group members leave this meeting convinced they have reached the best possible decision for the school district.

The details of this process of structured discourse are described in the appendix. While it is a critical process to use when trust levels among group members are low, it is also valuable whenever a leadership team needs to consider alternatives to problems that are both important and solvable.

Encouraging Productive Conflict in Leadership Teams

- The team must develop explicit norms for how they will engage one another in dialogue and debate.
- Participation in discussion improves when all team members receive relevant information in advance.
- Defining the nature and magnitude of the issue or problem is the first step for engaging in productive conflict.
- Until sufficient trust levels are established it is often necessary to assign team members to advocate for alternatives.

THE OFFICIAL TEAM LEADER'S ROLE

The leader of the team plays a crucial role in encouraging productive conflict within a school or district leadership team. Many school or district leaders desire to protect their team members from harm. Thus, they do not demonstrate the required restraint when people engage in conflict. They either attempt to avoid or stop the conflict from occurring. This does not send the message that conflict is a valid and valuable method for solving organizational challenges.

A team leader that wants to encourage productive conflict within his or her group must allow for resolution of conflicts to occur naturally. On the other hand, if the conflict becomes more about the individuals than the issues, the leader must intervene and refocus the discussion. Relationship conflict is detrimental regardless of the type of task a team is performing (Jehn, 1995).

Another action the team leader must take is to model the appropriate conflict behavior. More specifically, the leader must disagree with others while confirming their competence. The leader must attempt to see issues from others' perspectives and communicate an open and accurate perception of these perspectives.

Furthermore, the team leader must keep an open mind, changing his or her initial conclusions and positions when others' information, rationale, proof, and logical reasoning are persuasive and convincing.

In teams that avoid conflict, it may be necessary to extract the buried disagreements within the team. This "mining for conflicts" requires bringing forth sensitive issues and forcing team members to work through them. It is far better for the team leader to address the tough issues by acknowledging the unsaid. Skirting real issues by avoiding them will not help the team confront the reality of their current situation.

Lastly, the authority hierarchy among the members of a leadership team influences the quality and quantity of communication among group members. High-authority team members like a superintendent or assistant superintendent do most of the talking.

Furthermore, most of the messages delivered by team members are directed at those in high-authority positions. In other words, low-authority members often do not communicate messages directly to one another during a group meeting.

In addition, high-authority leadership team members frequently hesitate to reveal their vulnerabilities. On the other hand, because they fear evaluation by those with formal authority, low-authority group members avoid taking risks, speak superficially, and avoid candor in their remarks.

These hierarchical patterns of interaction thwart attempts at productive conflict. The team leader must serve to neutralize the "pecking order" if productive conflicts among all group members are to occur.

Official Team Leader's Role in Encouraging Productive Conflict

- The team leader must demonstrate restraint when productive conflict occurs.
- The team leader must model appropriate conflict behavior.
- When necessary, the team leader must bring conflicts to the "surface."
- It is the team leader's role to neutralize the "pecking order."

Feeling confident they have benefited from everyone's ideas, the leadership team can now collectively commit to team decisions. Collective commitment is the subject of the next chapter.

6

ESTABLISHING COLLECTIVE COMMITMENTS

All for one and one for all.

—Alexandre Dumas

Dr. Sampson has been the assistant superintendent for the Brownstone School District for the past six months. During this time period, he carefully assessed all aspects of the district's curriculum and instruction program. One of his conclusions is that the current process for developing curriculum guides is not effective. More specifically, the methods used currently result in curriculum guides that contain an unrealistic number of instructional objectives. Furthermore, these objectives are not sequenced or organized in a logical progression.

After discussing this matter with the superintendent, Dr. Sampson develops a new set of procedures designed to improve this situation. It takes him about two months, but eventually he is very pleased with the explicit nature of the process, including the new templates to be used. He believes the principals and curriculum supervisors will share his enthusiasm and will appreciate his efforts.

In preparation for the curriculum revision activities that will be occurring during the upcoming summer months, Dr. Sampson presents the information to all of the members of the administrative team. He carefully explains the new process, making sure to stress the advantages it will provide for the teachers and students in the school district. He concludes his presentation by asking for feedback and questions. He receives neither.

Two curriculum areas were due for revision during this summer. The first was the district's kindergarten through fifth grade math curriculum. This committee is chaired by Mrs. Olson, one of the elementary school principals. The second is the middle school science curriculum. This committee is chaired by Mr. Pinter, the district science supervisor.

It is standard procedure in the school district for the committee chair to submit the completed curriculum guide to the assistant superintendent prior to it being placed on the agenda for board of education approval. When Dr. Sampson receives the results of the committee's work, he is deeply disappointed. It turns out that both committees followed the old process and used the old templates to complete their task. Dr. Sampson immediately summons each committee chair to his office for an explanation.

First, he meets with Mrs. Olson. She explains that she was under the impression the change was to take place with curriculum developed during the next school year. It is clear to Dr. Sampson that based on her reaction she was not purposefully disregarding the new procedures. She did not use the process because she was not clear about the expectations.

Next, he meets with Mr. Pinter. As it turned out, Mr. Pinter received a lot of negative feedback from the middle school teachers about the new process and procedures. They believed the old method was effective, and it took them less time to complete it. Under pressure from these teachers, Mr. Pinter allowed the teachers to use the old method.

After expressing his disappointment and anger to Mr. Pinter, Dr. Sampson asked him why he didn't attempt to convince the teachers of the value of the new procedures. As it turns out, Mr. Pinter shared the feelings about the process that the teachers had expressed. With all of the other competing priorities his department faced, he just didn't see this as the "hill to die on" at this moment in time.

Dr. Sampson is completely frustrated by this situation. Neither curriculum document has been completed the way he expected it to be done. With all of his time and effort designing and presenting this new method, the district's curriculum and instruction program is no better than it was before. This is an example of the type of results that occur when a school or district leadership team does not adhere to the principle of establishing collective commitments.

DEFINITION OF COLLECTIVE COMMITMENT

Collective commitments in leadership teams are established when *team members make a decision they all accurately understand and then agree to move forward with the complete support of every member of the team.* Collective commitment cannot be achieved if leadership team members are unclear about what is being committed to. To achieve this clarity requires teams to avoid assumptions and ambiguity.

Furthermore, after engaging in productive conflict team members must end their advocacy role and publicly pledge to support the actions decided upon by the team. Leadership teams that are characterized by making collective commitments:

- have clear directions and priorities,
- use the phrases we, us, and our instead of I, you, and they,
- align group efforts around common objectives,
- move forward without hesitation.

Some decisions do not require the collective commitment of leadership team members. For example, when decisions are about matters that do not require committed action by most team members or

when decisions are so simple that coordination and understanding of
the actions required among team members is easy, a collective commitment is usually not necessary. Decisions needing to be made
quickly are also not going to be made collectively.

Collective commitments should be made for those things that
are complex, important, and require a commitment for follow-
through from most (or all) group members. Changing the district's
process for evaluating professional staff or deciding how the district will engage in professional development activities are two examples of topics requiring a collective commitment.

Important Points Regarding Collective Commitments

- Clearly understanding agreements is necessary for establishing collective commitment.
- Team members must publicly pledge their support for their
  team's decision.
- This process should only be used for those decisions that are
  important, complex, and require commitment for follow-
  through from most (or all) group members.

THE IMPORTANCE OF COLLECTIVE COMMITMENTS

Collective commitments are essential when teams are expected to
follow through on decisions made. However, as was illustrated in
the example at the beginning of this chapter, members of a leadership team can delay (Mrs. Olson) or sabotage (Mr. Pinter) the
implementation of what were thought to be shared commitments.
This results in both a lack of organizational improvement and a decrease in the trust levels among team members.

In addition, without establishing collective commitment, leadership team members frequently do not have clarity regarding direction and priorities. Without this clarity, team members make decisions and take actions they believe are helpful to the organization.

In reality, these actions often pull district resources in different, if not conflicting, directions. Aligned around collective commitments, team members and the organizations they lead are more likely to make steady progress toward their goals.

Importantly, when a leadership team fails to achieve clarity and buy-in from all of its members, those that report to their respective leaders will frequently clash. Typically this happens because individuals receive directions different from those provided to colleagues in other schools or departments.

Individuals in different schools and departments end up doing things differently. Yet they each believe they are doing those things correctly. When other staff members within the school or district do not do something they perceive to be the correct way, staff members question those individuals' motives or competence.

What may begin as a small gap between understandings among members of a leadership team can become major discrepancies by the time it filters down to the level of the staff members in departments or schools. This can severely damage the overall level of morale in the organization.

A summary of the Importance of Collective Commitments

- The sabotage or delays associated with a lack of buy-in keep an organization from continuously improving.
- Clear direction and priorities result in a more effective use of resources.
- Small gaps of understanding at the top frequently become large gaps in understanding among school or department members.

ESTABLISHING COLLECTIVE COMMITMENTS

There are multiple methods for making decisions. Each method of decision making inspires a different degree of commitment to the implementation of the actions associated with that decision from the members of a leadership team. Furthermore, each decision-making method is appropriate for different circumstances.

One option is for team members to provide input to the person on the team with the highest level of authority. This individual can then consider the input provided and make a final decision. This method is most appropriate for situations in which time constraints are a major factor.

While efficient, this method frequently results in team members displaying minimal ownership for the implementation of the actions associated with that decision. Furthermore, this approach may lead to competition among team members as they attempt to influence the official team leader (Levi, 2007).

Another possibility is for team members to cast votes. In this case the majority opinion becomes the decision. This method is a quick one for obtaining all of the team members' opinions on an issue. It is an appropriate method for making decisions that are not controversial and do not require extensive coordination for the implementation of the actions related to those decisions.

While continuing to be efficient, this method often promotes ownership exclusively among the group members voting in favor of the decision. Even more troubling is the fact that those who "lost" the vote may develop resentment toward the other members of the team.

The third decision-making option is the pursuit of consensus. Importantly, the type of consensus sought by a dynamic leadership team is not one in which everyone fully agrees. This level of agreement is difficult, if not impossible, for a leadership team to achieve. Pressed for time and representing a wide variety of viewpoints, wants, and needs, the pursuit of perfect consensus will typically result in team members experiencing frustration while the team's actions are unnecessarily delayed.

The types of consensus dynamic leadership teams strive for when making their decisions are those for which team members:

- had an adequate opportunity to clearly state their position,
- perceive that their viewpoints have been both heard and understood,
- can accurately rephrase, interpret, or summarize the decision made by the group.

A potential disadvantage to the consensus approach to decision making is the amount of time this method typically requires. Decisions made through a consensus approach take more time than other decision-making methods.

On the other hand, the extra time required to make a consensual decision may greatly reduce the time needed to implement it (Johnson & Johnson, 2006). Regardless, if there is an urgent need to make a decision the consensus method is typically not a viable alternative.

An advantage to the consensus approach is that making decisions through this approach forces all team members to exert a great deal of psychological energy. This is important because the greater the amount of effort that goes into making a decision, the greater the ability that decision has to influence the attitude of the person making it (Cialdini, 2007). In other words, if a team member puts forth a great deal of effort to make a decision, then he or she will have a higher level of commitment to that decision.

In sum, whenever decisions will have a significant impact upon team members, a high level of coordinated action will be required for effective implementation. If there is sufficient time, then a leadership team should employ a consensus approach to decision making.

Even when leadership teams make decisions through the consensus approach, it is completely possible they will not have considered all of the potential consequences. As a result of fixating on only one or just a few alternatives, the group may reach premature agreement on their final decision. A second-chance meeting is one way to avoid hasty decisions and further increase member buy-in (Johnson & Johnson, 1994).

If time allows, once the leadership team has reached preliminary agreement on the best decision, they should hold a second meeting within a forty-eight- to seventy-two-hour time period. During this time between meetings, leadership team members have an additional opportunity to reflect upon any of their remaining concerns.

At the second meeting, team members are provided with the opportunity to further express their remaining doubts and criticisms. Having provided this opportunity, team leaders can be certain that ample time has been provided for team members to express themselves both fully and truthfully.

Consensus types of decision-making methods combined with second-chance meetings increase the "buy-in" for decisions made by leadership team members. To cement commitment, team members must publicly state their willingness to give a decision a fair trial for a predetermined period of time.

The reason for making a public commitment is that whenever a person makes a commitment that is visible to others, there arises a drive to maintain behavior consistent with that commitment (Cialdini, 2007). Public commitments become long-lasting commitments.

One way of ascertaining public commitment is requiring team members to declare their support. To begin the process of declaring their support, each team member states an answer to the following three questions:

- Have I clearly stated my position on this issue during our previous discussions?
- Have I been heard and understood by the members of the team?
- Do I understand the option declared as the decision?

If the answer to any of these questions is a no, then that team member must share his specific concern with the team for additional problem solving.

If the answers to the above questions are yes, then the team member is expected to support the implementation of the team's decision. One method for declaring support for the implementation of a decision is requiring each team member to state the actions they will take in order to support the implementation of the decision. This may be done either orally or in writing.

Either way, collate the content of these statements and distribute them to all of the team members. This written declaration of support will serve as a public record of team members' commitments. Having made these commitments and gone on record as doing so, team members are highly likely to behave in ways consistent with the implementation of the team's decision.

A Summary of Establishing Collective Commitments

- A consensus style of decision making is important, but perfect consensus is impossible.
- Second-chance meetings help avoid premature closure.
- As a last step, responsibilities must be clarified and a public declaration of support by each team member must be made.

THE OFFICIAL TEAM LEADER'S ROLE

In order to establish collective commitments among the members of a leadership team, members must listen carefully and communicate effectively. The team encourages this behavior by establishing and enforcing a few basic guidelines.

First, team members must be encouraged to clearly and logically present their opinions. However, they must also be required to listen to other members' reactions and consider them carefully before continuing to press forward with their own point of view. Occasionally the leader may need to interrupt a discussion to encourage a team member or members to paraphrase their understanding of others' responses.

Sometimes group members will change their mind simply to reach agreement and avoid conflict. The team leader must emphasize to team members that when they are attempting to establish a collective commitment, they must support only those positions that they will be able to live with.

If it is important enough to become a collective commitment, it cannot be decided on by majority voting, averaging, or other forms of decision making. This will be especially tempting when discussions appear to have reached a stalemate.

Similarly the team leader must guard against team members "going along" with an idea with the implicit idea being that they will expect support on another issue. This is just another form of barter and compromise that undermines the quality of decision making.

The team leader needs to listen carefully for underlying assumptions and rationales. He or she needs to go beyond what is said to get at the meaning and feelings buried within those words. If the leader believes these assumptions and rationales need to be brought to the surface, he or she should tactfully inquire about them.

At some point, the leader may need to push for closure on an issue. When the discussion appears to be circular with no new information being provided, the leader must attempt to integrate the best arguments presented by all of the team members.

This must be done in a way that is not perceived as the leader being overly specific or controlling about the purpose, goals, and approach. When the leader's actions are perceived in this way they are likely to gain compliance to "their" purpose while losing commitment to the team's purpose. This is especially true at the beginning of a team's efforts when all eyes and ears are keenly attuned to how the leader will use authority with the team.

A Summary of the Official Team Leader's Role in Establishing Collective Commitments

- The group leader must model and facilitate the use of effective communication skills.
- The leader must not allow the group to achieve premature closure on an issue.
- If assumptions need to be stated explicitly, the leader must surface them.
- If an issue is going in a circular direction, the leader must press for closure.

Following the guidelines presented in this chapter will result in leadership teams that establish collective commitments. These commitments are characterized by a clear decision that has the sufficient level of "buy-in" necessary for carrying out assigned responsibilities. Once a collective commitment has been established, the team will be able to engage in holding themselves and their teammates accountable. This topic is the subject of the next chapter.

7

DEVELOPING MUTUAL AND INDIVIDUAL ACCOUNTABILITY

The honor of one is the honor of all.
The hurt of one is the hurt of all.

—Creek Indian creed

The leadership team of South Smithtown School District has established a common goal of requiring teachers to move from an emphasis on behavioral objectives toward an emphasis on the "big ideas" in the curriculum. One of the objectives to be met as part of this goal was the required use of a new lesson-planning format.

Several of the principals in the district encountered resistance from their staff members as a result of this decision. Their respective staffs had been using the old model for many years and had grown very comfortable with using it to plan their instruction. However, these principals gently but firmly continued holding the expectation that their staff members would follow this new format.

The challenges to their decision only mounted when several of the teachers discovered that one of the principals from a different school in the district let her staff make the decision to use either the new or the old model of lesson planning.

The principals that "held the line" were furious with their colleague. Through her actions she had undermined their ability to follow through with an agreed-upon team decision. They understood the temptation to give in to the pressure, but this was a commitment everyone understood and accepted.

At the weekly leadership team meeting, the principals challenged their colleague's actions. After listening to her state her reasons for why she had changed her mind and then acknowledging the difficulties associated with her circumstances, the rest of the team let her know that they expected her to do her part to fully implement the group's decision.

They coached her to own responsibility for her actions and assisted her in creating strategies for overcoming the resistance she was experiencing. The time for debate and discussion had ended. Now everyone on the team was expected to follow through.

She apologized to the team and stated her intention to rectify the situation in her school. The team then moved on to a new agenda item. The superintendent of schools never had to say a word.

DEFINING ACCOUNTABILITY

Many believe that accountability only arises when something goes wrong, or when someone wants to pinpoint the cause of a problem. This viewpoint represents a past-oriented, blame-centered perspective of accountability. Leadership teams must abandon this definition if they hope to move beyond fear and blame toward embracing responsibility.

Accountability in leadership teams consists of two separate, yet related, dimensions. First, in dynamic leadership teams members demonstrate individual accountability. *Individual accountability is a team member's sense of personal responsibility to do his or her best in order to help the team succeed.* This includes making, keeping, and answering for personal commitments. Without individual accountability among leadership team members, the possibility of social loafing increases.

Social loafing is the reduction of individual contributions when people work in groups rather than working alone (Levi, 2007). Related to the problem of social loafing is the concept of "free riders." Free riders are individuals who perform little in a group because they do not believe their individual efforts are important, and they know they will receive their share of the group's reward regardless of their efforts (Sweeney, 1973).

In order to avoid the phenomenon known as social loafing, members of the team must be required to complete identifiable individual tasks. Furthermore, it must be necessary for team members to work in a coordinated manner in order to achieve team success. Lastly, team members must receive accurate feedback on the extent of their contributions to the group.

Second, in dynamic leadership teams members demonstrate mutual accountability. *Mutual accountability is the team members' willingness to challenge one another on performance or behaviors if what a member is either doing or failing to do is or could interfere with the efforts of the team.* This attitude reflects the higher degree of commitment found among members of dynamic leadership teams.

Groups that embrace the type of accountability described in this chapter have interactions that are characterized by:

- tactful questioning of one another's approaches,
- regular and thorough reporting of results,
- ownership for circumstances and outcomes,
- high levels of specific, constructive feedback,
- high expectations for the performance of each team member.

IMPORTANCE OF ACCOUNTABILITY
TO LEADERSHIP TEAMS

There are at least two reasons why mutual accountability is critical to the success of leadership teams. First, under conditions in which accountability is high, group members develop more positive and cooperative relationships (Johnson & Johnson, 2006). Second, in situations characterized by mutual accountability team members are more committed to their group obligations than they are to concerns about their personal welfare (Lencioni, 2002).

BARRIERS TO MUTUAL ACCOUNTABILITY

Mutual accountability is a concept that is both threatening and foreign to most educational leaders. Typically educational leaders understand and abide by the need to be individually accountable for the results of their respective schools or departments. However, adding the dimension of mutual accountability threatens the simplicity and security of individual control and consequence management.

Most school-based or departmental-level leaders have come to depend upon the concept of only being responsible for their part of the organizational system. For example, a high school principal is likely to believe he or she is responsible for the results achieved by the school they lead and not the results obtained by other schools in the district. As a result educational leaders do not have experiences with mutual accountability to which they can relate.

Mutual accountability can also be uncomfortable because it may require challenging a peer on his or her behavior. There is a tendency to want to avoid these difficult conversations. Leaders that avoid having difficult conversations about accountability may do so out of fear of damaging interpersonal relationships.

However, when team members do not hold each other accountable for keeping commitments, relationships among group members eventually deteriorate (Johnson & Johnson, 2006). The reason for this deterioration in relationships is that group members eventually come to resent those they perceive as not living up to their responsibilities.

As the standards of the group erode, anger and frustration are likely to mount. In addition, those who are doing their best to keep the commitments may begin to reduce their efforts toward task completion because they do not want others to take advantage of them (Levi, 2007).

On the other hand, holding each other accountable reflects team members' respect for one another. Holding each other accountable symbolizes the high expectations team members have for one another's abilities and behaviors. It is a compliment to hold high expectations for a team member.

Great leadership teams understand the need to push past both their intra- and interpersonal discomfort with mutual accountability. A leadership team will not have long-term success if it does not embrace both individual and mutual accountability. When everyone understands a problem or situation and then treats it as both their own and the team's, positive results happen.

Key Points Related to Accountability

- High-performing leadership teams demonstrate high levels of both individual and mutual accountability.
- While threatening and foreign to educational leaders, a high level of mutual accountability is critical to the success of a leadership team.
- Mutual accountability can improve the quality of relationships among leadership team members.

DEVELOPING ACCOUNTABILITY

If the action plan generated for achieving the expected outcomes associated with a collective commitment is clear, then the need for mutual accountability will become evident. More specifically, an action plan with clearly defined responsibilities, specific timelines, and valid measures of success compels team members to realize that without coordinated efforts, the team cannot succeed.

Related to this will be the enhanced sense of individual accountability. If a team member clearly understands what they are expected to do, by when it must be done, and how success in taking those actions will be evaluated, then they are responsible for their actions. However, there are additional steps a leadership team can take to increase the probability that accountable behaviors will be exhibited by team members.

To encourage accountability, a leadership team must keep their action plans visible. One means of doing this is to provide a copy of the action plan to each team member. Even better is the prominent display of one enlarged copy of the plan in the team's regular meeting location.

As steps in the action plans are completed, they can be marked off. Doing this makes it possible for the team to know if a step has not been completed. Then the team can take action before any shortcomings become overly problematic. Team members will have difficulty ignoring their responsibilities when they are being kept at the forefront of the team's attention.

A second step leadership teams can take to encourage accountability among team members is to regularly require reporting on plan-related actions. As one part of each leadership team meeting, every team member reports on the actions he or she has taken, or failed to take, toward completing assigned responsibilities.

This progress review provides the forum for team members to question one another's actions. Of course, this will only happen if team members have trusting relationships, embrace productive conflict, and are committed to achieving the team's goals.

To encourage individual accountability, leadership team members' performance evaluations should include both individual and team performance measures. For example, information on the individual's level of active participation in team discussions and demonstrated ability to follow through on team tasks should be included when conducting the formative and summative evaluations of a leadership team member. Including this information in the evaluation process will both reduce social loafing and provide information that can be used to identify the assistance needed for specific individuals (Levi, 2007).

Traditionally, the employee's supervisor conducts the performance evaluation. However, teamwork evaluations should be performed by more than just the supervisor (Lawler, 2000). The reason for this change is that only team members can accurately evaluate an individual's role in the team.

This becomes difficult when team members' information could be used for high-stakes decisions. Team members may resist being honest if they believe the evaluation will be used for more than feedback or team development (Lawler, 2000).

An option that provides valuable feedback but does not connect directly to formal evaluation is the use of a 360-degree team-member feedback exercise. The objective of this exercise is to provide team members with peer-based, focused, and direct feedback that they can use to improve their team performance.

The procedure involves having each team member privately write the answers to two questions about the other members of the team. The questions are:

- What is _____'s single most important contribution to the effectiveness of the team?
- What is _____'s single most important characteristic that detracts from the effectiveness of the team?

Going in a round-robin sequence, each individual reads his or her answer to the first question. There are no questions or discussion at this point. After everyone has shared their responses, the individual receiving the feedback responds to what was said. At this point, he or she can ask for clarification or provide a reaction to the information shared.

This same sequence is followed for the second question. To conclude the segment for the individual receiving the feedback, that person should share with the rest of the team one or two key points they will work on in order to improve their performance as it relates to team effectiveness. The sequence then continues with the rest of the team members.

A Summary of Developing Accountability in Leadership Teams

- Accountability is an attitude that emerges in response to high trust levels, productive conflict, and collective commitments.
- To encourage accountability, team members must be clear about individual responsibilities and expected results.
- Action plans related to collective commitments must be kept at the forefront of the group members' attention.
- Team members' performance evaluations should include information on both team and individual behaviors.

THE OFFICIAL TEAM LEADER'S ROLE

Paradoxically, true mutual accountability frequently does not require the participation of the team leader. If an individual is a team player, the peer pressure and disdain for letting down peers will be more motivating than any fear of administrative punishment.

Just as in the example at the beginning of this chapter, sometimes the most important step the team leader can take is to encourage and allow the leadership team members to serve as the first and primary mechanism for accountability. This requires restraint for leaders used to being the sole source of team discipline.

This does not mean the team leader never holds leadership team members accountable. On the rare occurrence in which team members fail to hold one another accountable, the team leader must not hesitate to hold someone accountable for their behaviors or performance. By doing this, the leader is communicating the message to team members that accountability has not been relegated to a consensus approach.

Indeed, accountability is a shared team responsibility. However, it must be clear that it is one that the team leader will assume if it becomes necessary. It has been my experience that if team members know the leader has the courage to and will hold them accountable, they will be less hesitant to do it themselves.

The team leader must avoid offering all of the solutions for solving the problems related to poor performance or inaction. Doing this removes ownership from team members. It is far better for the team leader to provide the direction and coaching necessary for team members to come up with their own solutions.

Lastly, team leaders must hold themselves to the same standards of accountability as everyone else. Blaming the inability to complete tasks on issues like local politics, lack of resources, or government regulations provides team members with the excuse to do the same. A team leader cannot ask others to consistently rise above difficult circumstances in an effort to complete assigned tasks if they do not demonstrate a willingness to do it themselves.

A Summary of the Official Team Leader's
Role in Promoting Accountability

- Allow the team to be the first and primary source of accountability.

- If the team fails to hold a member accountable, the leader must take this role.
- Resist the temptation to take ownership for generating solutions to solve the problem.
- Model willingness to rise above circumstances to achieve results.

If the members of a leadership team are not held accountable for their actions, their attention will likely shift back to the needs of their own respective schools or departments. Encouraging accountability as described in this chapter is critical for maintaining a focus on collective results. Focusing on collective results is the synergistic behavior that is the subject of the next chapter.

8

FOCUSING ON COLLECTIVE RESULTS

Teams get results.

—Katzenbach and Smith

The tension from the headache was so extreme, he felt like his head was going to pop off his shoulders. As he left this morning's leadership team meeting, he had developed so much stress in his neck and shoulders that he was beginning to feel nauseous. As the new principal of a middle school, Dr. Jackson never anticipated either this level or this source of frustration.

He wondered if the real problem was that his expectations were unrealistic. He believed that individuals both should and would put aside their own goals in order to meet the needs of the organization. As educators, wasn't everyone supposed to be in the profession to provide the best possible education for children? The answer to this question was not so clear now that his school's leadership team was experiencing some difficulties.

Recently several of his school's leadership team members' personal ambitions appeared to be a higher priority to them than the collective mission they had worked so hard to establish only several months ago.

Mrs. Franklin, the assistant principal in charge of discipline, clearly had ambitions to be a high school principal. Currently in her area of the state, school districts were looking for principals with demonstrated experience implementing technology initiatives. Also highly desirable was experience managing new construction projects and developing supportive technology infrastructure.

As a result, Mrs. Franklin kept pushing for projects that would demonstrate her ability to complete these tasks. These were not the school's top priorities, but they were what she needed to have on her resume to get hired for the position she desired.

Mr. Randall, the chair of the math and science departments, was trying to complete his doctoral dissertation. Having gone through this process, Dr. Jackson was sensitive to the time and effort required to complete this task. However, it seemed that all Mr. Randall wanted to do was design and conduct his study.

The leadership team had decided that the topic of differentiating instruction was the most important focus for improving teaching and learning in their school. While Mr. Randall's work on promoting teacher professionalism was interesting, it did not directly address this need.

Dr. Jackson wondered if he was the only one willing to subjugate his own goals and interests for the benefit of the team. The individualistic behavior Mr. Randall and Mrs. Franklin were displaying was causing the school's improvement efforts to stagnate. Dr. Jackson was at a loss for getting these team members to make the collective results achieved by the group more important than each individual member's personal goals. He knew he needed to do it, he just did not know how.

DEFINING A FOCUS ON COLLECTIVE RESULTS

Schools and districts improve when individuals place the needs of the larger organization above their personal needs. This is not a natural human tendency. People are commonly inclined to look out for their own self-interest and self-preservation. Becoming a dynamic leadership team requires team members to overcome this strong, natural tendency to primarily look out for themselves.

Teams that focus on collective results are those for which *the primary objective of all of the team members is maintaining a focus on the achievement of the group's goals.* Groups that maintain their focus on collective results are characterized by:

- avoiding distractions such as ego, personal or career development, and salary;
- briefly enjoying their successes and temporarily lamenting their failures;
- making genuine sacrifices for the good of the team with the only expectation of repayment being enhanced team success.

IMPORTANCE OF FOCUSING ON COLLECTIVE RESULTS TO LEADERSHIP TEAMS

When educational leaders, like those in the example at the beginning of this chapter, stop caring about the results achieved by the leadership team, they usually start caring about something else. That something else is frequently personal ego, career advancement, salary, or school/departmental needs.

Whatever this replacement focus becomes, it diverts attention and energy away from the team's pursuit of collective results. When this happens teams lose focus on achieving the goals designed to address the most important priorities for the larger organization. Subsequently the overall organization fails to grow and improve. As a result, the school or district underperforms even though some aspects of the system may be thriving.

A second major concern related to a lack of focus on collective results is that processes are necessary but not sufficient. A team can implement a range of elaborate processes to achieve a task. However, if the team does not focus on the results of their actions, they cannot know the impact caused by those actions. Impact on student development should be the primary reason the leadership team exists.

Key Points Related to Collective Results

- It is not human nature to place the needs of the team above individual needs.
- Members of dynamic leadership teams maintain focus on achieving the team's collective goals.
- When team members lose focus on collective results, this focus is frequently replaced with attention being paid to other needs.
- When something other than collective results becomes the focus, the overall organization stagnates, even though some departments or schools may be doing well.
- By itself teamwork is not a fully legitimate goal; the leadership team exists to achieve results.

DEVELOPING A FOCUS ON COLLECTIVE RESULTS

If focusing on individual wants and needs is a strong and natural human tendency, then a purposeful effort will be required in order for team members to maintain focus on achieving collective results. High levels of individual and mutual accountability will certainly help. However, emphasis on achieving individual responsibilities associated with the team's task will not be enough to keep team members focused on the results related to the team's common goals.

So how can team members maintain focus on the achievement of collective results? First, the team must regularly update and review measures that describe results. Second, team rewards and/or recognition must be provided contingent on the achievement of the team's desired results.

The connection between the impact of the team's actions and the accomplishments achieved must be clear. One way to do this is to develop and update the team's "scoreboard." This scoreboard can be any visual display that serves as a means for tracking team progress.

To create a worthwhile display it is necessary to gather high-quality data. Thus, specified team members must know what data to collect and how often it is to be collected. Furthermore, they should understand why the data is being collected and how it should be compiled.

A check sheet is a simple data collection form used to answer the question "How often are certain events happening?" A check sheet is created by:

1. defining exactly what is to be observed;
2. determining the time period during which the data will be collected;
3. designing the form and making sure all of the team members can use it;
4. collecting data consistently and honestly;

Suppose a leadership team has a goal of reducing the number of special-education referrals in the school district. To achieve this goal, the leadership team institutes common formative assessments, intensive teacher training, and new forms of supplementary services. To collect the data necessary for tracking progress, the team creates the check sheet shown in table 8.1.

At specified intervals (in this case monthly), team members provide this data to one team member. This team member compiles the data and creates a visual display for the team to review. For data being collected on a regular schedule over an extended period of time, it is especially effective to have a permanent visual displaying the compiled data in the regular team meeting room.

Table 8.1. Check Sheet

Month	Parent Referral		School Referral		Other Referral		Eligible for Services		Declassified	
	Total	%	Total	%	Total	%	Total	%	Total	%
September										
October										
November										
December										
January										
February										
March										
April										
May										
June										
Summer										

Now let's say this same team wants to track the total number of school referrals by month. A run chart is a line graph used to monitor the behavior of selected characteristics over time. Data points plotted over time allow the leadership team to identify trends. More specifically, the team can see when shifts and changes occur and then take timely action to stop problems or capture and preserve good changes.

A run chart is constructed by plotting data points on an x-y axis in chronological order. Measurement data are represented on the vertical (y) axis, and time or sequence is represented on the horizontal (x) axis. A marked point indicates the measurement taken at one point in time. Based on the information presented in figure 8.1, the leadership team would likely conclude that as the school year is progressing, the number of referrals initiated by school staff is decreasing.

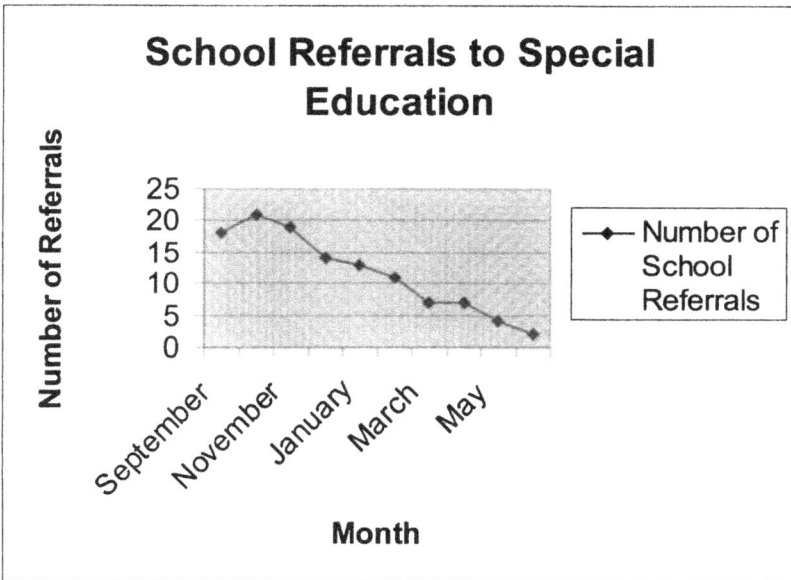

Figure 8.1. School Referrals to Special Education

A histogram shows the distribution of data by demonstrating how continuous measurement data is clustered and dispersed. Histograms are especially helpful when the team wants to examine the distribution and the spread of the data. They show the frequency of an occurrence and the dispersion between the highest and lowest values.

The horizontal axis of the histogram represents the range of data. The vertical axis represents the number of data points at each interval. Each column represents an interval within the range of data. The team looking at the data in figure 8.2 would likely conclude that while the number of referrals initiated by staff is decreasing as the school year progresses, the number of parent-initiated referrals is not.

One of the most critical aspects of tracking team progress is keeping the process simple. Collecting data requires both time and the use of resources. Keep the process restricted to the collection and analysis of the information necessary to assess team progress.

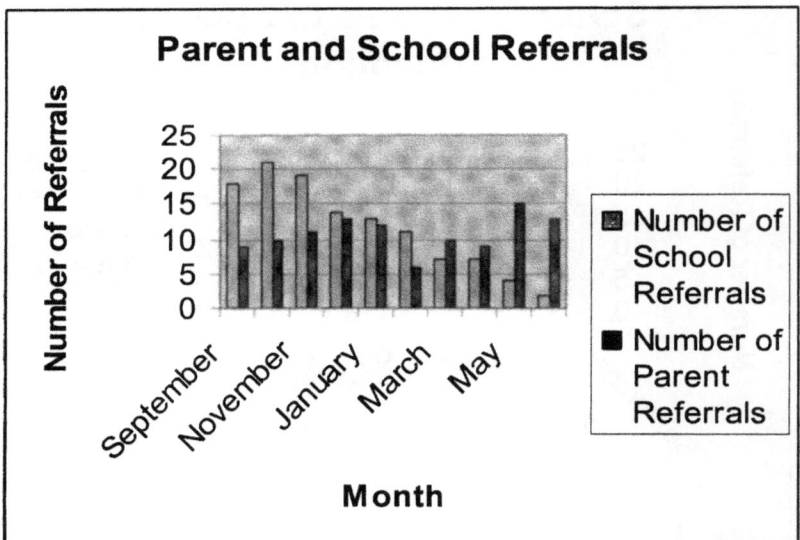

Figure 8.2.   Parent and School Referrals

In addition, if it is at all possible, the data collection should be designed to fit into the normal workflow.

The school district's reward system provides an important vehicle for encouraging a leadership team to maintain its focus on collective results. Team rewards have the potential to influence the motivation of individual team members, the level of coordination in the team, and the quality of the group process (Levi, 2007).

A major form of reward is the compensation provided to employees. Usually school systems provide pay to employees based on individual performance and longevity with the organization. In the case of administrators, an additional criterion for determining pay is the individual's position in the organization's hierarchy. None of these criteria encourage cooperation and teamwork.

It is unrealistic to believe that team-based methods for providing compensation will become the primary method for rewarding employee performance. Furthermore, sole use of team rewards has potentially undesirable effects. More specifically, only using team-based rewards may encourage social loafing and discourage the motivation of high-performing employees (Dematteo, Eby & Sundstrom, 1998).

Teams that are rewarded for a mix of individual and team performance perform better than teams rewarded for solely individual or team performance (Fan & Gruenfeld, 1998). Thus, a hybrid approach that combines team and individual rewards appears to be the best solution.

In addition to a salary increase based on individual performance, members of a leadership team could be provided with additional compensation for achieving the team's goals. While the pay for individual performance may vary, every member of the team will receive the same reward for achieving the team's goals. However, the provision of any compensation for achieving the team's goals will depend upon the team's ability to demonstrate the expected results. Insufficient collective results equal no additional compensation for any leadership team member.

Nonfinancial recognition programs may also be used to reward successful team performance. Although these programs are a valuable way of acknowledging effort beyond expectations, these programs are useful to supplement, but not substitute for, financial reward systems (Lawler, 2000).

If recognition is provided to the members of a leadership team, it should be provided contingent on meeting the expected performance standards, and it should be something desired by the members of the team. Presentation of the reward should be public and should be done in close time proximity to the achievement being recognized.

Key Points Related to Focusing on Collective Results

- Regularly tracking and reviewing team progress toward goal achievement encourages maintaining a focus on collective results.
- Combining individual with team reward systems will require team members to focus on both individual and collective achievement.
- Financial compensation is superior to nonfinancial recognition when the desired outcome is enhanced leadership team performance.

THE OFFICIAL TEAM LEADER'S ROLE

To establish a focus on collective results by a leadership team, the group leader must establish the appropriate expectations. One way to do this is by the group leader's actions.

If team members believe the group leader values something other than the team's collective results, they will take this as permission to do the same thing themselves. The team leader must act in a manner that makes it clear that the most important focus must be on the achievement of the team's goals.

Second, the group leader cannot excuse away shortfalls in team performance. Talking as though results are desired but failing to achieve them will not sustain teams, nor will it improve schools. The group leader must avoid publicly placing blame on any team members, but must make it clear that results matter. Focusing on outcomes helps create and sustain the performance ethic necessary for becoming a dynamic leadership team.

Finally, the team leader must praise only those behaviors that contribute to the achievements of the team's desired results. In order for praise to promote a focus on collective results, statements must meet two conditions. First, the praise must be provided to the team as a whole and not to individual team members. Second, the praise must be contingent on meeting a previously established standard of performance. Praise for simply investing time and effort sends the message that the results are not so important after all.

A Summary of the Official Team Leader's Role in Promoting a Focus on Collective Results

- The team leader must model the desire to achieve collective results.
- The team leader must not make excuses for poor performance.
- Praise must be used to reinforce desired organizational behaviors.

The first three chapters of this book described why leadership teams are necessary, who should serve on them, and what they should accomplish. Chapters 4 through 8 described the synergistic team behaviors necessary for acting dynamically. The last chapter of this book addresses leadership team meetings, the context in which most of these activities will occur.

LEADERSHIP TEAM MEETINGS

School leaders who were recruited, trained, and rewarded for running a tight ship and always being in control must learn and relearn much if schools are to be led in participatory ways.

—Lorraine Slater

Imagine a leadership team meeting that is engaging, relevant, and interactive. Does your mental image include members of a team sharing progress toward commonly held goals and objectives? Are team members sharing their top priorities for the upcoming week and then developing a meeting agenda based upon what everyone is currently working on? Are the meeting participants engaged in candid, focused dialogue on instructional and achievement issues? Does the meeting end with everyone clarifying their roles and responsibilities as well as whom they must share information from the meeting with?

If your experiences are similar to mine, this description is more of a fantasy than a reality. Instead, most of the leadership team meetings I have participated in have been "information dumps" with interactions between group members being tightly controlled by the official leader of the group.

This type of meeting is characteristic of the command and control mentality associated with traditional school leadership. However, the twenty-first century approach to organizational behavior calls for collaboration (Slater, 2005). The implementation of shared leadership models requires school leaders to develop a set of talents and skills not traditionally essential to their role. Furthermore, this style of leadership runs counter to the training and experience of most school administrators (Haskin, 1995).

As Beatty (2000) suggested, perhaps school leaders need to begin to concern themselves less with running "tight ships" and more with creating tightly knit communities. For a leadership team, meetings are the primary context in which a sense of community and cohesion is established. In other words, to achieve the goals and behaviors described in this book, leaders will have to change the way they meet as groups.

MEETING TYPES

Not all meetings are held to achieve the same objectives. Thus, there must be different types of meetings with different structural elements for meeting these varied purposes. The five types of meetings a leadership team should engage in are the start-up, strategic, regular, professional development, and social meetings.

Start-Up Meetings

If this is the first meeting of a leadership team, it is essential for it to be carefully structured. For most school or district leadership teams, at least some of the members will come to this meeting with undeveloped social relations. Furthermore, group members will have an ambiguous understanding of the norms the group will use to operate. Decisions made during the initial meeting of a team will establish a trajectory on which members will stay for an extended period of time (Hackman, 2002). To avoid wasting time and effort, it must be the right trajectory.

The aim of the start-up meeting is to begin the process of establishing social relations, and to clarify the group's norms. The first activity of a start-up meeting should focus on getting team members acquainted with one another. The exercise titled "Getting to Know Me" can be used to accomplish this goal. It takes five to ten minutes per participant and requires no materials. The steps in the activity are:

1. Beginning with the official team leader, have everyone introduce themselves and then share the answer to the following three questions:
   a. where they grew up,
   b. how many siblings they have and where they fall in the sibling order,
   c. how their parents would describe them as a child.
2. After everyone has had a turn, ask team members to share what they learned about one another that they did not already know. This reinforces the purpose of the exercise and allows for closure to the conversation.

After completing the "Getting to Know Me" activity, the group should engage in the process of establishing conflict norms. The procedures for accomplishing this goal are described in the Positive Conflict Norms activity located in the appendix.

The final activity for the start-up meeting should focus on the clarification of the team's basic operating principles. The objective of this activity is the achievement of clarity among team members for how everyone will deal with one another on a regular basis. This activity takes between forty-five and sixty minutes and requires access to a large writing surface. To complete this activity, the team will discuss and come to resolution on the following issues (and any others appropriate to that particular team):

- Meeting times—When and where will meetings occur?
- Attendance—What are legitimate reasons for missing meetings?
- Promptness—How important is it for team members to be on time to meetings?
- Disruptions—When is it acceptable for the meeting to be disrupted?
- Membership—When will membership on the team be expanded or contracted?
- Evaluation—How will the team's task work and teamwork be evaluated? How will individual team members' performance be evaluated?
- Team leadership—If or when will the role of the team leader rotate?
- Communication between meetings—What is the preferred method for communication between meetings and how should these methods be used?
- Sharing information—How will input from non-team members be obtained? How will the team decide what to share with nonmembers? What, if anything, should never be shared?

As agreements are reached, they are recorded on a large writing surface. After all of the responses have been completed, the official team leader leads the team members in a review of the agreements. The purpose of this review is to ensure everyone understands the substance of each agreement. Team members' questions are encouraged at this time. After the meeting, written copies of the agreements are distributed to each team member.

In close proximity to (if not a part of) the start-up meeting will be the team's first strategic meeting. However, only select aspects of the strategic meeting will be appropriate at this point. More specifically, the team should engage in the activities designed to create the team's initial collective goals.

Strategic Meetings

There are two major areas of focus for strategic meetings. The first is reflection and learning from the team's previous efforts. Reflecting on both the individuals' and the team's efforts will enable the team to continuously learn and improve as they work toward new goals.

Therefore the second focus for the strategic meeting is the establishment of the team's common and compelling purpose. More specifically, at the end of each strategic meeting the team will emerge with action plans for achieving new "POWERful" goals.

The frequency of these meetings varies because they are only held when new goals must be established. The majority of activities to be accomplished in a strategic meeting can be completed in one day. However, a second-chance meeting should occur on another date in close proximity to this one. The time required for this second meeting will be thirty minutes to one hour.

The following activities serve as the agenda for a leadership team's strategic meeting. For the first ten to fifteen minutes of the meeting, group members engage in a "team review." More specifically, the team conducts a review to determine any lessons learned from the completions of their last set of goals. The focus of this review is the task work completed by team members. The quality of teamwork is the focus of the second activity.

Prior to this meeting, each team member will have completed and submitted to the team leader a team self-assessment form (located in the appendix). The team leader comes to the meeting prepared to share the compiled results. After sharing these results, the group will spend between fifteen and twenty minutes engaged in an open discussion focused on teamwork strengths as well as identifying areas needing improvement.

After focusing on the quality of teamwork, the focus shifts to the quality of individual members' contributions. The previously described 360-degree team-member feedback exercise is the method used to achieve this task.

The remainder of the strategic meeting focuses on identifying collective goals. Sequentially using the brainstorming, guiding questions, dot voting, decision matrix, fist-to-five, and action planning activities, the team develops two goals. The first goal focuses on the most important action the leadership team can take to improve academic achievement. The second goal focuses on the most important action the leadership team can take to improve the quality of instruction.

Regular Meetings

Group cohesion generally has a positive impact on group performance. One variable that determines the level of cohesion in a group is the amount of time the group spends together. More specifically, groups that spend more time together tend to be more cohesive (McKenna, 1994). Of course, this assumes the meetings are positive and productive.

Enhanced group cohesion is one reason why regular meetings should be held frequently and on a regularly scheduled basis. These meetings typically last between sixty and ninety minutes and should include the following elements.

Every regular meeting begins with a team warm-up. These are short icebreaker activities designed to continue the process of getting team members more acquainted with one another. After reviewing progress toward completion of the action plans developed during the strategic meeting, the team will conduct a round-robin share.

The content of this round-robin sharing is the team members stating their top two or three priorities for the upcoming week (or period between regular meetings). Each team member takes less than one minute to quickly describe the activities they intend to focus on accomplishing. It is at this point that the meeting agenda is developed.

Working collaboratively, team members develop a meeting agenda based on the previously articulated team members' priorities and how effectively the team is performing toward meeting its goals. Doing this after the progress updates and the round-robin share ensures that the substance of the meeting is relevant.

For the next twenty to thirty minutes, the team engages in discussion focused on the agenda items. This is a highly focused discussion limited to the agenda items. Once the discussion has ended, it is time to clarify the commitments made.

To clarify the commitments made, the team leader facilitates a dialogue to determine what has been agreed upon during the course of the team discussion. If there is no consensus, the team leader facilitates further discussion in order to eliminate discrepancies. Once agreement is reached, either the team leader or a designee records these commitments and distributes them to team members soon after the meeting.

Related to clarifying commitments is the process of communicating the substance of those commitments. More specifically, team members decide which, if any, of the commitments and agreements reached need to be communicated to others outside of the team. Team members are charged with responsibility for sharing this information within a given time period.

As a final activity, team members evaluate the quality of the meeting. First, each team member comments on what the team did well during the course of this meeting. Next, each team member comments on what the team could do better the next time they meet.

Professional Development Meetings

When professional development occurs with the entire team, the group develops a shared mental model. Group members become co-oriented to the nature of the training topic and develop the same meaning for any vocabulary used.

In addition, team members experiencing common professional development experiences can hold one another accountable for transferring what was learned to the school or district. Furthermore, these team members can provide support and answer questions when implementation issues arise.

For the reasons cited, leadership teams should engage in common professional-development experiences. More specifically, at least annually leadership team members must gather for a common learning experience. Ideally this common learning experience will relate to the achievement and instructional goals of the school district.

Regardless of the content selected, team members must have a voice in selecting the topic. If team members have a say in the content for the experience, they will approach the activity as something that is meaningful and relevant.

Social Meetings

The purpose of social meetings is to foster team spirit and build interpersonal connections among team members. When successful, these meetings strengthen the team's morale, increase trust, and develop group identity.

Therefore, on occasion the team should have open-ended meetings simply to promote social relationships. These meetings can be as complicated as retreats or as simple as having lunch together. The main point is that team members should engage in non-work-related activities that encourage team members' continued learning about one another. Getting to know colleagues on a personal level promotes interpersonal bonds and social cohesion among team members.

RESISTANCE

If the methods described for conducting meetings are new, the team leader must be prepared to encounter resistance. Leadership team members may object to the amount of time they are being directed to spend attending meetings. This is a serious miscalculation of the cost-benefit relationship between time and teamwork.

I have found it effective to address this matter before it becomes an issue. This has been done by explaining up front that there is a tremendous amount of time and energy already being wasted on organizational politics, lack of clear understanding of roles and responsibilities, competition between schools and departments, and rarely achieving closure on critical organizational issues.

The types of meetings described in this chapter offer a practical solution to an existing problem. I "sell" these meetings as an eventual time-saver that will increase the overall effectiveness of the school or district. In essence, this approach takes the "I don't have enough time" issue off the table before anyone can object.

Another objection is the belief that time can't be spent in meetings because there is "real work" that needs to be done. If you consider the nature and outcomes associated with typical leadership team meetings, this is an understandable objection. However, operating as a team in the manner described throughout this book is all about getting things done.

While it does take time to achieve the status of becoming a dynamic team, once that has been accomplished the team will achieve greater results in less time. It is a slight leap of faith for team members, but it is one that is necessary for crossing the abyss between the traditional and the dynamic leadership team. Leaping this abyss to become dynamic leadership teams will result in a shift of the focus for school and district personnel from "mine" to "ours." Ultimately all of our students will be the beneficiaries of this new way of thinking and acting.

APPENDIX

BRAINSTORMING

Objective: To generate and select viable alternatives for addressing an issue or problem. In the case of developing "POWERful" goals, it is answers to the two questions articulated in chapter 3.
Time required: Twenty to thirty minutes per issue, problem, or question.
Materials required: A writing surface all team members can view. Additional materials may be necessary depending upon the option selected for sharing ideas.
Procedure:

1. Write out and post the issue(s) or question on a whiteboard or chart paper.
2. Explain to the team that the task is to generate as many alternatives or answers as possible for solving this issue/ answering this question.
3. Review the following guidelines for this activity with the team.

   a. To effectively brainstorm we will:
   - Aim for lots of ideas—the more the better.
   - Avoid evaluating ideas during this activity.
   - Build on and add to others' ideas.
   - Avoid repeating or trying to sell an idea.
   - Welcome and record all ideas.
4. There are several activities that can be used at this point to guide the sharing of ideas. These include:
   a. *Free-for-all*: Team members rapidly share ideas. As each idea is verbalized, it is recorded. Several recorders each standing at a different chart can help to speed the process. The facilitator simply calls upon a group member and directs that response to be written by one of the recorders. As that recorder is writing the statement, the facilitator calls upon another group member and directs that response to a different recorder for writing. Another option is to provide team members with self-stick notes. Each participant is to write one idea per self-stick note. Having ideas written on self-stick notes makes sorting and organizing ideas easier and promotes anonymity.
   b. *Round robin*: Going in sequence, each team member shares an idea. Participants are allowed to pass when it is their turn if they have no idea to share. If the team has more than ten members, it should be broken down into smaller groups of no more than five or six individuals. Because it equalizes participation, this is an especially effective method to use with groups that typically interact in a hierarchical manner.
   c. *Solution trade*: Have team members sit in a circular pattern. Provide each individual with five blank index cards. Ask each team member to generate one idea and write it on one index card. Next, each team member passes his or her index card clockwise to someone else on the team. This person reads the idea and attempts to build on it. On a new

index card, they write down either this "piggybacked" idea or a brand-new idea. Team members will continue passing for approximately five minutes. Once the time is up, the facilitator collects all of the cards and records the ideas (except duplicates) for the rest of the group to view.

d. *Centerpiece*: Individuals in teams of three to five fold a piece of paper into six boxes. Individuals write one idea in a box on their piece of paper. Next, the paper is placed in the center of the table and someone else's paper is taken. This process is continued until all of the boxes are filled. The facilitator records all of the ideas generated (except duplicate ideas) so they may be viewed by the rest of the team.

GUIDING QUESTIONS

Objective: To provide direction for the leadership team as they narrow the options generated during brainstorming.

Time required: Twenty or more minutes, depending on the number of options being explored.

Materials required: Flip-chart page with the guiding questions written on it and markers.

Procedure:

1. Review the guiding questions with team members. Clarify any questions about the substance of each question. The guiding questions for this activity are:

   • *Does successful completion of this option require the efforts of all of the leadership team members?*

   • *Is it possible to observe and count the result of this option?*

   • *Is it possible for us to implement this option?*

   • *Does the option draw your energy and attention?*

   • *Do we have evidence that implementation of this option is necessary in our district?*

- *Do we have evidence that implementation of this option has the potential to make a significant difference in the quality of education for our students?*

2. Proceed to evaluate each of the options against the first question. If a no answer is provided for an option, then that option is eliminated.

3. Continue sequentially evaluating each of the remaining options against each of the guiding questions.

4. After all of the questions have been answered, the only options remaining will be those meeting the POWERful criteria.

DOT VOTING

Objective: To narrow a list of alternatives.

Time required: Ten to fifteen minutes for each set of brainstormed ideas.

Materials required: Colored sticky dots (all the same color) and a flip-chart paper that lists the alternatives generated during the previous brainstorming session.

Procedure:

1. Divide the number of alternatives by three (round up to the nearest whole number). That is the number of sticky dots each group member is to receive.

2. Explain to group members that each dot represents one vote.

3. Allow group members to place their dots next to the ideas they favor most.
   a. They may be distributed in two ways. One per idea or if the group agrees, two or more dots may be placed on one item.

4. Revise the list by eliminating items that received few or no votes.

5. If the revised list is still larger than two to four alternatives, repeat the process with the remaining items. Use different-colored dots.

6. Continue this process until you reach the top two to four alternatives.

DECISION MATRIX

Objective: To evaluate potential options against criteria.
Time required: Thirty to forty-five minutes.
Materials required: Large writing surface and writing implement, paper, and pens or pencils.
Procedure:

1. Write the alternatives being considered on the left-hand side of the writing surface.
2. Identify criteria that are important to the team. Examples include time required, cost, staffing required, long-term impact, and learning and training necessary. Make sure the criteria are clearly stated and understood by all group members. Create columns for each of these criteria.
3. Determine if each criterion is equal in value. If some are more important than others, they can be weighted.
4. Using a scale of zero (not met at all) to five (fully met), each team member should privately score each potential solution against the criterion. They should proceed vertically and not horizontally.
5. Each person should total the score for each idea. If any criterion is weighted, they must make sure to multiply the score by that factor. For example, if five were the value assigned and the weight for that factor was double, the value would actually be ten ($5 \times 2 = 10$).
6. Average individual scores to obtain a team score. The option with the highest total is the strongest match to the criteria.

FIST-TO-FIVE

Objective: To ascertain individual team members' opinion regarding an option under consideration.

Time required: Five minutes. May be more depending upon the individual responses.

Materials required: A piece of flip-chart paper and felt-tip markers.

Procedure:

1. Explain the options team members have for expressing their opinion.
   a. Five fingers—I fully support this option.
   b. Three fingers—I am willing to support this option, but I still have concerns.
   c. Fist—I will not support this option because I have serious concerns.
2. State the option being considered.
3. Have team members express their level of support for this option by having them hold up the corresponding number of fingers. If everyone holds up a five, the activity if finished. If not, proceed to step four.
4. Provide those displaying three fingers with the opportunity to voice their concerns. Also ask those displaying a fist to explain why it is not possible for them to support this option. Record all of these reasons on a piece of flip-chart paper.
5. Facilitate a discussion in which the team members try to address the stated concerns. Attempt to resolve the concerns through group problem solving.
6. After the team discussion, call for an additional fist-to-five vote.

ACTION PLANNING

Objective: To develop a plan of action for the team that clearly states the actions, responsibilities, timelines, and evaluation criteria as they relate to implementing the agreed-upon POWERful goals.

Time required: Thirty to sixty minutes per goal.

Materials required: Large writing surface with a writing implement. Divide this writing surface into the columns *Action Steps*, *Responsibilities*, *Timelines*, and *Evaluation*. For each goal, one action plan will be developed.

Procedure:

1. Facilitate a discussion of the various action steps that must be completed to ensure the successful implementation of the team's goal. Write each one in sequential order under the column labeled *Action Steps*.
2. Starting with the first task, identify the person who will take leadership responsibility for this action step. Record his or her name under a column labeled *Responsibilities*. Clarify and list who else will be involved in completing this action step.
3. Ask the person with leadership responsibility to state when the task will be started and when it will be completed. Other team members can provide input as necessary. As the dates are decided, they are recorded under a column labeled *Timelines*.
4. Facilitate a discussion for how the team will know the task has been successfully completed. Once established, write this under a column labeled *Evaluation*. Repeat steps two through four with each action step, filling in each column on the chart.

LEADERSHIP TEAM SELF-ASSESSMENT FORM

Directions: For each of the items below, please provide a 1 to 4 rating by circling the response that indicates your level of agreement with the statement.

1 = strongly disagree   2 = disagree   3 = agree   4 = strongly agree

Section 1—Trust

1. Group members freely admit mistakes and weaknesses.	1	2	3	4
2. Group members are honest and straightforward in their communications.	1	2	3	4
3. Group members freely share information and data.	1	2	3	4
4. Group members are loyal to those that are not present.	1	2	3	4

Section 2—Productive Conflict

5. Group members actively seek out the perspective and opinions of all group members.	1	2	3	4
6. Group members state their opinions on issues without holding back due to fear of retribution or rejection.	1	2	3	4
7. Group members freely express support for ideas as well as doubt and objections.	1	2	3	4
8. Two-way communication occurs between all group members.	1	2	3	4
9. Critical issues and topics are placed on the "table" for discussion.	1	2	3	4

Section 3—Collective Commitment

10. As a team we have clear direction and priorities.	1	2	3	4
11. In our discussions, we regularly use the phrases we, us, and our instead of I, you, and they.	1	2	3	4
12. As a team we are moving forward without unnecessary delay.	1	2	3	4

Section 4—Mutual Accountability

13. We tactfully question one another's approaches.	1	2	3	4
14. We regularly and thoroughly report on results.	1	2	3	4
15. We take ownership for circumstances and outcomes.	1	2	3	4
16. We provide each other high levels of specific, constructive feedback.	1	2	3	4
17. We hold high expectations for the performance of each team member.	1	2	3	4

Section 5—Focus on Results

18. We avoid distractions such as ego, personal or career development, and salary.	1	2	3	4
19. We briefly enjoy our successes and temporarily lament our failures.	1	2	3	4
20. We make genuine sacrifices for the good of the team with the only expectation of repayment being enhanced team success.	1	2	3	4

ESTABLISHING POSITIVE-CONFLICT NORMS

Objective: To establish clear expectations for how leadership team members will engage one another in discussion and debate.
Time required: Forty-five minutes.
Materials required: A large, clearly visible writing surface for recording ideas; pens or pencils; and sheets of composition paper.
Procedure:

1. Using a team as an example, the leader introduces the idea of conflict norms.
   - *We have all been a part of a group that has experienced conflict. While not always treated this way, conflict is necessary for us to grow, learn, and improve as a school (or district). It is not a matter of if we will have conflict as a team, but how we will manage our conflicts when we have them. The purpose of this activity is to develop expectations for how we will treat one another in our effort to obtain the positive benefits associated with conflict.*
   - What are some of the behaviors, both positive and negative, that you have experienced in a group experiencing conflict? (Record the responses on a T-chart.)

Example

Table A.1.   Team Behaviors

Positive Team Behaviors	Negative Team Behaviors
* Discussing the real issues	* Giving in to avoid conflict
* Focusing on problems/not people	* Meeting after the meeting
* Giving support after being heard	* Avoiding the important issues

2. Initiate a group discussion about the messages the behaviors listed in each column send to members of the team.
3. On a piece of chart paper, brainstorm possible agreements for promoting positive conflict. Continue adding possible

agreements until the team members believe they have exhausted the possibilities.

4. Have team members divide a piece of paper so that it results in two columns of equal size. Next, inform group members that they have 100 points. Explain that they may spend these 100 points among each of the sample agreements listed. As points are "spent" on one agreement, they are to be subtracted from the total of 100. Points represent the importance the value has for the spender.

5. After having team members complete the task individually, team members should share their scores with a group of two or three group members. The discussions that often follow this activity help to clarify thinking about the agreements. After this small group sharing, the personal points are distributed again. The team leader then collects all of the sheets and tallies how many points were spent on each item. Only the second score should be counted. You will then end up with the team's agreements for promoting productive conflict.

6. It is often necessary to remind team members of the agreements they have established. Much like students, adults need occasional reminders of the norms they have agreed to follow. Reminding team members about the agreements they have made can occur verbally at the beginning of a team meeting. It can also be distributed in written form to each group member.

DEFINING THE ISSUE

Objective: To ensure all team members share a common understanding of the nature and magnitude of a selected problem or issue.
Time required: Twenty to thirty minutes.
Materials required: A writing surface all team members can view.

Procedure:

1. As a team, brainstorm on a piece of chart paper or a whiteboard a series of statements describing the issue or problem. Attempt to make these statements as clear and concrete as possible. Continue this process until the team members run out of statements.
2. Remove statements that require resources or authority beyond the control of the group.
3. Restate each statement so that it includes a description of both the desired and actual state of affairs. Avoid arguing or attempting to solve the problem at this point.
4. Choose the statement group members agree is the most accurate description of the issue or problem. This may require combining aspects of various statements into one.

STRUCTURED DISCOURSE

Objective: To engage in dialogue about the positive and negative aspects of alternatives.
Time required: Sixty to ninety minutes.
Materials required: None.
Procedure:

1. Utilizing the alternatives selected, propose two or more possible courses of action (e.g., reducing class size by hiring new teachers or purchasing more technology to be used for classroom instruction).
2. Form subgroups and assign them the responsibility for advocating in favor of their assigned alternative. Regardless of their personal beliefs or feelings, these subgroups are responsible for presenting the best possible case for their assigned position.

3. Provide time for each subgroup to research its position and prepare a persuasive presentation designed to convince the other group(s) of the validity of their position.
4. Have each subgroup present their case to the rest of the team.
5. Have subgroups reverse perspectives. At this point the groups switch roles, presenting the best possible case for the position they initially opposed. This is helpful for getting group members to see the advantages and disadvantages for each option without becoming too invested in one of the positions.
6. Have an open discussion in which team members argue their points of view and refute each other's positions.

360-DEGREE TEAM MEMBER FEEDBACK EXERCISE

Objective: To provide team members with peer-based, focused, and direct feedback they can use to improve their performance.
Time required: Ten to fifteen minutes per team member.
Materials required: Composition paper and writing implements.
Procedure:

1. Each team member is to privately write the answer for two questions about the other members of the team. They are:
   • What is _____'s single most important contribution to the effectiveness of this team?
   • What is _____'s single most important characteristic that detracts from the effectiveness of this team?
2. Going in a round-robin sequence, each individual reads his or her answer to the first question. There are no questions or discussion at this point.
3. After everyone has shared their responses, the leader responds to what was said. At this point, he or she can ask for clarification, or provide a reaction to the information shared.

4. Follow steps two and three for the second question.
5. Have the team leader share one or two key points they will work on for improving their performance as it relates to the team's effectiveness.
6. Continue this sequence with all of the members of the team.

REFERENCES

Beatty, B. (2000). The emotions of educational leadership: Breaking the silence. *International Journal of Leadership in Education*, 3(4), 331–57.

Cialdini, R. (2007). *Influence: The psychology of persuasion*. New York: Collins.

Cloke, K. & Goldsmith, J. (2005). *Resolving conflicts at work*. San Francisco: Jossey-Bass.

Collins, J. (2001). *Good to great*. New York: Harper Collins.

Connors, R., Smith, T. & Hickman, C. (2004). *The Oz principle: Getting results through individual and organizational accountability*. New York: Portfolio.

Covey, S. (2007). *The speed of trust: The one thing that changes everything*. New York: Free Press.

Dematteo, J., Eby, L. & Sundstrom, E. (1998). Team-based rewards. Current empirical evidence and directions for future research. *Research in Organizational Behavior*, 20, 141–83.

Fan, E. & Gruenfeld, D. (1998). When needs outweigh desires: The effects of resource interdependence and reward interdependence on group problem solving. *Basic and Applied Social Psychology*, 20(1), 45–56.

Hackman, J. R. (2002). *Leading teams: Setting the stage for great performances*. Boston: Harvard University Press.

Haskin, K. (1995). A process of learning: The principal's role in participatory management. *American Educational Research Journal*, 35(1), 3–31.

Jehn, K. (1995). A multimethod examination of the benefits and detriments of intra-group conflict. *Administrative Science Quarterly*, 40, 256–82.

Johnson, D. & Johnson, J. (1994). *Leading the cooperative school*. Edina: Interaction Book Company.

Johnson, D. & Johnson, J. (2006). *Joining together: Group theory and group skills*. Boston: Allyn and Bacon.

Katzenbach, J. (1998). *Teams at the top*. Boston: Harvard Business School Press.

Katzenbach, J. & Smith, D. (2003). *The wisdom of teams*. New York: Harper Collins.

Lawler, E. (2000). *Rewarding excellence: Pay strategies for the new economy*. San Francisco: Jossey-Bass.

Lencioni, P. (2002). *The five dysfunctions of a team*. San Francisco: Jossey-Bass.

Leucke, R. (2004). *Creating teams with an edge: The complete skill set to build powerful and influential teams*. Boston: Harvard Business School Publishing.

Levi, D. (2007). *Group Dynamics for Teams*. Thousand Oaks: Sage Publishing.

Levine, J. & Choi, H. (2004). Impact of personnel turnover on team performance and cognition. In E. Salas & S. Fiore (Eds.) *Team cognition: Understanding the factors that drive process and performance* (pp. 153–75). Washington, DC: American Psychological Association.

McKenna, E. (1994). Business psychology and organizational behavior. Hillsdale, NJ: Lawrence, Erlbaum.

Moreland, R. & Levine, J. (1989). Socialization in small groups: Temporal changes in individual-group relations. *Advances in Experimental Social Psychology*, 15, 137–92.

Slater, L. (2005). Leadership for collaboration: An affective process. *International Journal of Leadership in Education*, 8(4), 321–33.

Smith, K. & Berg, D. (1987). *Paradoxes of group life*. San Francisco: Jossey-Bass.

Steiner, I. D. (1972). *Group process and productivity*. New York: Academic Press.

Sweeney, J. (1973). An experimental investigation into the free rider problem. *Social Science Research*, 2, 277–92.

ABOUT THE AUTHOR

Matthew Jennings is currently the superintendent of schools for the Alexandria Township Public School System. Prior to serving in this position, Dr. Jennings served as an assistant superintendent of schools, a director of student services, a supervisor of curriculum and instruction, and a classroom teacher. He earned his master's degree and doctorate in educational administration from Rutgers University.

In addition to presenting at numerous state and national conferences, Dr. Jennings has served as an organizational behavior consultant to school districts throughout New Jersey. He works as an adjunct professor for Rutgers University, where he teaches courses on curriculum development, school administration, and the supervision of instruction. His work has been published in *Kappan*, *Preventing School Failure*, *The New Jersey English Journal*, *Channels*, and *The Writing Teacher*. His most recent publication, *Leading Meetings, Teams and Work Groups in Schools and Districts*, was released by the Association for Supervision and Curriculum Development in June of 2007.

When he is not spending time with his wife MaryAnn, his children Ryan and Tara, and their dog Amber, Dr. Jennings enjoys time at the beach, competing in triathlons, and Rutgers football games.